COMMON-
SENSE
EVIDENCE

THE EDUCATIONAL INNOVATIONS SERIES

The Educational Innovations series explores a wide range of current school reform efforts. Individual volumes examine entrepreneurial efforts and unorthodox approaches, highlighting reforms that have met with success and strategies that have attracted widespread attention. The series aims to disrupt the status quo and inject new ideas into contemporary education debates.

Series edited by Frederick M. Hess

OTHER BOOKS IN THIS SERIES

The Strategic Management of Charter Schools
by Peter Frumkin, Bruno V. Manno,
and Nell Edgington

Customized Schooling
Edited by Frederick M. Hess and
Bruno V. Manno

Bringing School Reform to Scale
by Heather Zavadsky

What Next?
Edited by Mary Cullinane and
Frederick M. Hess

Between Public and Private
Edited by Katrina E. Bulkley, Jeffrey R. Henig,
and Henry M. Levin

Stretching the School Dollar
Edited by Frederick M. Hess and Eric Osberg

*School Turnarounds: The
Essential Role of Districts*
by Heather Zavadsky

Stretching the Higher Education Dollar
Edited by Andrew P. Kelly and Kevin Carey

Cage-Busting Leadership
by Frederick M. Hess

*Teacher Quality 2.0: Toward a New
Era in Education Reform*
Edited by Frederick M. Hess and
Michael Q. McShane

*Reinventing Financial Aid: Charting a
New Course to College Affordability*
Edited by Andrew P. Kelly and
Sara Goldrick-Rab

The Cage-Busting Teacher
by Frederick M. Hess

*Failing Our Brightest Kids: The Global
Challenge of Educating High-Ability Students*
by Chester E. Finn, Jr. and Brandon L. Wright

*The New Education Philanthropy:
Politics, Policy, and Reform*
Edited by Frederick M. Hess and
Jeffrey R. Henig

Educational Entrepreneurship Today
Edited by Frederick M. Hess and
Michael Q. McShane

*Policy Patrons: Philanthropy, Education
Reform, and the Politics of Influence*
Megan E. Tompkins-Stange

*Convergence of K–12 and Higher Education:
Policies and Programs in a Changing Era*
Edited by Christopher P. Loss and
Patrick J. McGuinn

*The Every Student Succeeds Act: What It
Means for Schools, Systems, and States*
Edited by Frederick M. Hess and Max Eden

Letters to a Young Education Reformer
by Frederick M. Hess

*Bush-Obama Education
Reform: Lessons Learned*
Edited by Frederick M. Hess and
Michael Q. McShane

*Education, Equity, and the States:
How Variations in State Governance
Make or Break Reform*
Sara E. Dahill-Brown

*International Perspectives in
Higher Education: Balancing
Access, Equity, and Cost*
Edited by Jason D. Delisle and Alex Usher

COMMON-SENSE EVIDENCE

The Education Leader's
Guide to Using
Data and Research

NORA GORDON | CARRIE CONAWAY

HARVARD EDUCATION PRESS
Cambridge, Massachusetts

Paperback ISBN 978-1-68253-505-9
Library Edition ISBN 978-1-68253-506-6

Library of Congress Cataloging-in-Publication Data

Names: Gordon, Nora, author. | Conaway, Carrie, author.
Title: Common-sense evidence : the education leader's guide to using data and research /
    Nora Gordon, Carrie Conaway.
Description: Cambridge, Massachusetts : Harvard Education Press, [2020] | Includes index.
Summary: "The book is a practical guide for education leaders (principals, superintendents,
    state education department staff, and officials) on using evidence to make decisions to guide
    improvement in their schools"— Provided by publisher.
Identifiers: LCCN 2020018504 | ISBN 9781682535059 (paperback) |
    ISBN 9781682535066 (library binding)
Subjects: LCSH: Education research. | Quantitative research. | Educational leadership. |
    School improvement programs.
Classification: LCC LB1028 .G624 2020 | DDC 370.72—dc23
LC record available at https://lccn.loc.gov/2020018504

Published by Harvard Education Press,
an imprint of the Harvard Education Publishing Group

Harvard Education Press
8 Story Street
Cambridge, MA 02138

Cover Design: Wilcox Design
Cover Image: © Maxkrasnov - Dreamstime.com

The typefaces used in this book are Minion Pro, Milo OT, Myriad Pro, and Trade Gothic

CONTENTS

Introduction 1

1 Turn Problems of Practice into Research Questions 9

2 Know Where to Find Useful Research Fast 29

3 Determine How Relevant and Convincing the Research Is 47

4 Understand What ESSA Says About Evidence (and What It Leaves Out) . . . 73

5 Build Evidence by Learning from Your Own Data 85

6 Interpret and Share Your Evidence 113

7 Build and Sustain Evidence Use in Your Organization 137

Conclusion 159

Further Readings 163

Notes 165

Acknowledgments 173

About the Authors 177

Index 179

INTRODUCTION

Using evidence to make decisions is common sense. Any education leaders worth their salt gather a body of information from multiple sources to shape their choices, from big decisions, like whether to change a mathematics curriculum or expand early childhood programming, to small ones, like how to differentiate instruction within a curricular unit. Research is often an important part of that body of information, but it's not the only component. Local values and perceptions matter. So do financial, legal, and other practical constraints that drive successful implementation.

The rhetoric around evidence in education, however, is anything but common sense. In discussions of evidence-based policy and practice, the word *evidence* is often used to mean a single piece of information from a single study. In contrast, the *Oxford English Dictionary* defines evidence as "Grounds for belief; facts or observations adduced in support of a conclusion or statement; the available body of information indicating whether an opinion or proposition is true or valid."

What's more, evidence-based policy takes too narrow a view of what constitutes important information, often limiting the evidence to studies with methodologies that can convincingly establish whether an intervention "worked." This narrow view of evidence permeates the federal Every Student Succeeds Act (ESSA) and constitutes some of the criteria for inclusion in the What Works Clearinghouse (WWC) sponsored by the US Department of Education's Institute of Education Sciences. But it leaves out a vast amount of valuable information, including what educators observe in their own situations. This limited approach also excludes other types of academic research, such as the brain science that helps us understand how people learn to read or qualitative work that helps explain why a policy or an intervention failed so we can improve our next attempt.

By dismissing the complexity of the challenges that education leaders face and instead promoting technocratic "evidence-based" solutions, education leaders become passive recipients of wisdom from the "experts" rather than key players in creating that wisdom. The reduced role of frontline educators in informing educational practice and policy is bad news for students, because only by testing ideas and learning from the results can organizations improve over time. And it's especially bad news for students whose families lack the resources to step in when schools fail them.

We've written this book in response to education leaders who tell us they don't want or need technocrats to tell them what to do. Instead, educators want to improve their schools using the best tools and information they can. Our book meets this authentic demand for evidence. We'll show you how to build research skills that will enrich and diversify the information you draw on. To build these skills, you will need to use the existing research base and learn from your own organizations' work. Common-sense evidence means using a wide variety of information sources in service of students—not using research for the mere sake of being perceived as evidence-based.

We are professional researchers, and we love working with people who want to lead with evidence and would like a little help in learning how. After years of formal training in statistics and research methods, we've each spent two decades conducting our own research, reviewing others' research, and trying to make sense of literatures full of contradictory findings. We have taught graduate and undergraduate courses in education policy, economics, and research methods, and we've spent a great deal of time helping professionals, including education practitioners, policy makers, and journalists, interpret research.

Our research colleagues produce work of great value, and we want to help education leaders benefit from this source of information. But as researchers, we also know the limitations of research. Education leaders need to learn how to determine how relevant and convincing the research is and build their own evidence to inform their work. Contrary to the prevailing wisdom, education leaders and practitioners can indeed engage with "real" research. They don't need to be spoon-fed oversimplified results. We ourselves rely on a streamlined, intuitive process in our day-to-day work, and we think educators can too. And the good news is this: the process relies far less on advanced statistics and more on common sense than you might expect.

THE REAL PROBLEMS WITH EVIDENCE USE IN EDUCATION

Advocates of evidence-based policy have lamented for decades that evidence isn't used enough to guide practice in education. To a degree, they have a point. A recent nationally representative survey of school and district leaders from the National Center on Research in Policy and Practice found that only about half of survey respondents agreed or strongly agreed with the statement "I find it valuable to consult education research" or "I look for research studies that might be relevant" when confronted with a new problem or decision.[1] And only 54 percent reported that they "conduct studies on programs we select and implement to see how they work" "often" or "all the time." But bemoaning the problem in light of these statistics misses two key points: the available evidence is less helpful than these advocates imagine, and leaders already use more evidence than the advocates think—just in different ways.

Much of the evidence often viewed as most rigorous isn't as helpful as it could be, because it is divorced from the actual needs of the field. This disconnect arises from the academic community's focus on a narrow, methodologically based definition of quality, which overvalues the technical aspects of research and undervalues relevance. In contrast, most of what we suggest in this book would not meet a top peer-reviewed academic journal's requirement for rigor. Don't get us wrong. All else being equal, we'll take greater methodological rigor over less. But rigor has its downsides. It can limit what you can evaluate, where you can evaluate it, and how applicable what you learn will be in a real-life setting.

One issue with rigor is that programs, often developed by nonprofits or other external vendors, are easier to evaluate rigorously than practices are. *Programs* are based on clearly defined protocols that all participants implement similarly, whereas *practices* are ideas about education that educators can customize to their settings.[2] If we only build evidence on programs, then a push for evidence-based practice morphs into a push for vendor-based practice. That push also leaves out core practices employed in every district—for example, what time to start the school day, how to configure grade spans across schools, and how to assign teachers to classrooms. Changes to these core practices could substantially improve outcomes, often at little additional cost.[3] Further, most research designs evaluate a given program or strategy as if it operates in isolation, when in reality many factors interact in the complex, social process of educating humans.

Rigorous evaluations require resources that many districts lack, such as access to a research professional with substantial expertise. Rigorous evaluations also require a large number of participants, and often a large number of schools. This means lots of research gets conducted in atypical contexts, so the findings might not easily translate to other settings. And when outside researchers, rather than education leaders, set the agenda, the outsiders are less attuned to real-world political and fiscal constraints, as well as how things are actually implemented.

All of these downsides suggest that the most rigorous research—the kind most people mean when they talk about evidence-based practice—is designed by and for researchers, rather than for practitioners. The supply of evidence is not meeting the actual demands of the field. So when practitioners say they see little value in research, who can blame them?

Furthermore, education leaders are already incorporating research into the body of information they are using to guide their work. They are just doing it in ways that are hard to observe—even for the leaders themselves—and they could be doing it more intentionally and efficiently. When advocates of evidence-based policy claim that educators don't use research, they have in mind what Carol Weiss, a scholar of research use, would call *an instrumental use of research*: actively consulting research to inform a decision.[4] But Weiss's work and many related studies have demonstrated that research also influences policy and practice conceptually—by shaping ideas and beliefs, providing frameworks for understanding, shifting the options under consideration, and altering the terms of debate.[5] Practitioners who use research in this way may not be able to provide specific citations to the individual pieces of research that have influenced their thinking. Indeed, they may not even realize that research is the source of some of their ideas. But its influence is there just the same. And while much of the existing academic research may miss the mark for education leaders' needs, the popularity of sources like Edutopia and EdReports suggests education leaders are hungry for information on topics related to real problems of practice.

But there's a big challenge. Education leaders are not typically trained in how to evaluate research evidence, let alone how to generate their own. Without building strong research skills, they may unintentionally be swayed by weak evidence, particularly when it confirms what they already believe to be true. Education leaders, like all other humans, are subject to cognitive biases that can limit the range and quality of information they use. Rather than searching rationally for information to answer our questions, we humans are hardwired to be more likely to notice information that aligns with what we already believe and to overlook or dismiss information that is inconsistent with our beliefs.[6] Recognizing this tendency—and knowing how to avoid it—helps leaders avoid being persuaded by faulty data and gain access to the full body of information on an issue, not just what they already believe to be true.

OVERVIEW OF THIS BOOK

In this book, we'll develop several case studies to show how expert leaders, who are novices to research, use and build evidence. We created these case studies from conversations we have had with education leaders throughout our careers. While none is based on any single educator's story, all the cases are based on real challenges we've seen educators face. They are meant to be realistic examples, rather than exemplars of best practice. We've constructed these examples to show leadership at the school building, district, and state levels, and on three topics (absenteeism, academic performance, and workforce development) to demonstrate how our principles apply across a variety of education settings and issues. We hope that you see a version of yourself and the challenges you face reflected in at least one of the cases.

First we'll introduce Superintendent Rebecca Sisti of the Lincoln School District. Chronic absenteeism rates in her schools—four elementary schools, a middle school, and a high school—are too high. She has been paying close attention to the average daily attendance rates for years, but until this measure was added into the state accountability system, she hadn't noticed how many students were missing 10 percent or more of the school year. The chronically absent students are missing at least eighteen days out of the year—on average, at least two days every month. That amounts to considerable academic content they never have the opportunity to learn. And now the chronic absenteeism rate counts as part of her ranking, and her schools are below average—some of them so far below that they're getting uncomfortably close to the state's criteria for putting a school into turnaround status. She needs to do something, but she doesn't know what. We will present Rebecca's challenges as a case study throughout the book to illustrate what leading with evidence looks like in practice.

We'll also develop the case of Maria Gonzalez, the math department chair in a large urban middle school. In the past few years, she has seen student performance on the state math test drop substantially between seventh and eighth grades. She wants to figure out how the teachers in her department can improve student performance on the eighth-grade exams. Finally, we've created a case around a chief state school officer. He has many rural districts in his state. He often hears from his rural superintendents about their troubles hiring teachers, especially the superintendents' inability to find teachers certified in special education, English as a second language, and physics. He doesn't know how widespread these problems are or what exactly his local leaders are doing to try to solve them—but he knows that they are spending a lot of time talking about it at their regional meetings.

This book provides concrete steps for seeking out and interpreting research, conducting your own studies, and integrating what you learn. Although we focus on how to use evidence for organizational improvement, we aren't asking you to sign on to a highly standardized or detailed continuous improvement system here. We want to make evidence use intuitive and accessible even to those who don't have the bandwidth for the most sophisticated systems. At the same time, many districts have found value in working with systems such as Plan-Do-Study-Act, the Data Wise Project, and improvement science, so we have structured our approach to be flexible and work in conjunction with them.[7]

We include suggestions to apply your learning at the end of each chapter in the book. The prompts will help you use evidence to think about a problem you face in your work. If you are reading on your own, we encourage you to take a moment and jot down some notes. Each prompt sets you up to continue to the next step. If you are using this book with a group or in a training session, these "Apply Your Learning" sections are good places where you can stop, individually reflect on what you have learned, and then discuss these ideas and findings.

We recommend reading the entire book to start, then returning to relevant chapters as you work. In the real world, this process will be much less linear. You will loop back to the beginning or go through a few steps multiple times, and sometimes you'll be working on multiple steps at once. The nonlinear progress of research makes the ordering of steps somewhat artificial, but the order presented in the book makes the most sense for understanding our approach.

In chapter 1, we start with your problem. We show how to turn a problem of practice into questions that research can answer. We explain why it's important to ask three kinds of questions—to diagnose the problem, assess implementation, and evaluate impact—even though evidence mandates often focus only on questions of impact. Chapter 2 shows how to get started looking for answers when your questions can be answered with existing research. We recommend initially looking for a big-picture overview and then turning to individual studies when you can't find an overview or when you need to dig deeper. Consider nonacademic sources, but follow the money to understand the source and any potential biases. We'll walk through resources like the WWC and Google Scholar and show how to find academic studies for free. When you do need to turn to an individual study, chapter 3 will show you how to pull key information out of it to determine how relevant and convincing the study is for your question. We explain why you don't need to read the entire study and show you what to look for. Chapter 3 also explains how to focus on practical significance without being blinded by claims about statistical significance or effect size.

We next turn from our view of what makes research relevant and convincing to how ESSA defines its levels of evidence. Chapter 4 tackles what ESSA says about evidence, as well as what it leaves out, including basic and qualitative research. It explains how ESSA's narrowest definition of evidence applies to relatively few schools and how the law tries to encourage school districts to continuously study their own efforts. Chapter 5 teaches just that: how to learn from your own data. We demonstrate how to make comparisons to answer your current questions, in your own situation, and how to combine comparisons to make them more convincing.

All these answers aren't helpful unless you can interpret and share what you learn, from the existing research and your own data, in an accessible way. Chapter 6 shows how to interpret and communicate your findings, using words and data displays. Still, you may still have some uncertainty. Where will the time come from? How will you get everyone on board? Chapter 7 explains how to build and sustain a culture of evidence use in your organization. Whether you are a beginner, an intermediate, or an advanced research user, you'll learn where to start and what options you have for promoting this culture.

While evidence is critical for improving education outcomes and increasing equity in education systems, it is—and should be—only one of many considerations in your decisions. In fact, that's exactly how our democratic system is designed. It's a feature, not a bug, of our educational system that leaders consider stakeholder perceptions, political concerns, financial constraints, and capacity as they do their work. The approach in this book acknowledges this reality so that you can use evidence in real life.

1

TURN PROBLEMS OF PRACTICE INTO RESEARCH QUESTIONS

Many leaders report struggling to find the right evidence to inform the problems they face. Here's why: leaders face problems, but researchers answer questions. But research can still be helpful in solving problems; you just need to know how to turn a problem into a question. This chapter shows you how to make this transformation. We also show you how to break your question into smaller parts narrow enough that research can inform them. In later chapters, we'll focus on applying evidence from your own or others' research to answer these questions.

USE EFFECTIVE QUESTIONS

Some questions are about underlying problems, and others are about strategies to address problems. We use *strategies* as an umbrella term for the programs, practices, interventions, policies, and any other actions taken by education leaders intending to improve outcomes. Most questions fall into one of three types: questions that diagnose problems, questions that assess the implementation of strategies aimed at solving those problems, and questions that assess the impact of those strategies. While you will customize your questions for different problems and strategies, the questions generally follow these basic templates:

- To diagnose the problem: Is the problem worse when ___ (or for ___)?

- To assess the implementation of a strategy: How would (or did) we implement the strategy, compared with the best-case scenario?

- To evaluate the impact of a strategy on the problem: How might (or did) the strategy change outcomes for us?

A disproportionate share of the evidence aimed at leaders and practitioners answers questions of the third type, about whether a strategy "works." But all three types of question are critical for leading with evidence. Even if a strategy is proven to help solve a specific problem, if that's not your problem or if you run into implementation issues, the strategy might not work for you.

Making questions narrow enough so that they can be answered (whether by you or by someone else) with data is often the hardest step. It helps to break the big question you care about into many narrower questions. The sidebar "Three Types of Research Questions" outlines the three question types, the broad questions pertaining to each type, and the narrower questions that flow from the broad ones.

Three Types of Research Questions	
BROAD QUESTION	**NARROWER QUESTIONS**
1. Diagnosing the problem	
Is the problem worse when _____ (or for _____)?	What is the best way to measure current outcomes? What are those outcomes now? What alternative explanations for this problem can we check? How convincing and relevant is this research finding (see chapter 3)?
2. Assessing the implementation of the strategy	
How would (or did) we implement the strategy, compared with the best-case scenario?	What is the strategy supposed to look like in best practice (the faithful-implementation scenario), and what would (or does) it look like in our setting? What are *all* the resources this strategy requires (e.g., space, scheduling, training, materials, budget, communications)? What can we monitor to see if we are on track?
3. Evaluating the impact of the strategy	
How might (or did) the strategy change outcomes for us?	How do the outcomes for the group that participated in the strategy compare with those for the group that didn't? And what alternative strategy (potentially just business as usual) did the nonparticipating group use? How convincing and relevant is this research finding (see chapter 3)?

ASK "HOW DO I KNOW?"

Some narrow questions seem easy or obvious, and it may be tempting to think that you already know their answers. We urge you to make it part of your routine to pause and ask, "How do I know that something I am pretty sure is true, or have always assumed is true, actually is true?" Questioning your own assumptions helps you fight the cognitive biases we all face—biases that can prevent you from digesting important new pieces of information. Asking "How do I know?" is a prompt to verify your assumptions with a concrete, objective source. It gives you the chance to notice that some pieces of "information" are less than objective, are not true in your situation, or don't speak to the claim at hand.

We're not alone in our love for this question. Systems improvement experts at Chapin Hall, a policy research institute at the University of Chicago, ground their technical assistance to child welfare agencies around teaching staff to ask the question "How do I know?" at every stage of their continuous quality improvement process.[1] In his book *When Can You Trust the Experts?*, one of our favorite reads on evidence in education, Daniel T. Willingham urges readers to "trace" what they think they know, as well as what experts vaguely assert. Carrie even developed the "How Do We Know" initiative for her state agency in Massachusetts, because she believed that if she could help educators answer that one question well, they could transform their practice.[2]

We recommend that you ask yourself, "How do I know?" at least twice. First, ask yourself, "How do I know that I am considering the relevant body of information?" You may have heard something from a colleague or read a blog post referencing a few new studies, but individual facts may be at odds with the fuller body of information available from research. You need to think about using all of what is known about a topic, rather than just what you've run across. Then, for any influential piece of information in that body, follow up by asking yourself, "How do I know that this is true?" Ask these questions when you are considering not just others' claims but also your own. Over time, a person's opinions can blur into assumptions that seem like objective facts. By subjecting your own beliefs to the same level of scrutiny you apply to others', you can keep the valuable information from your own experience and professional judgment in the mix.

UNCOVER THE PROBLEM

Defining the problem is a good first step in general—and when you are using research evidence. In a world full of product vendors and advocates hawking things that supposedly work but that solve problems you don't actually have, a clear understanding of your own problems can help block these distractions.

> As superintendent of Lincoln School District, Rebecca Sisti becomes aware of her problem when her state agency sends a preview ahead of the public release of the latest accountability data in late September. In her state, the chronic absenteeism rate is defined as the percentage of students who are absent on 10 percent or more of their days of enrollment in the district. She sees in the report that the Hillside and Lemont Elementary Schools have alarmingly high chronic absenteeism, at 17.8 and 16.2 percent of students. That's high enough to drag down those two schools' ratings in the state's latest accountability system, and the other schools in her district aren't far behind.
>
> Rebecca forms an elementary school task force on chronic absenteeism for the Lincoln School District. The group is composed of staff representatives from each elementary school and the central office. She asks Erin Frazier, the counselor at Lemont, to lead the task force and to be ready with recommendations by the end of November, shortly before the next districtwide professional development day.
>
> "I know you can't plan a complete overhaul in that timeframe," Rebecca says, "but I want us to take at least some concrete steps with our students this academic year. The recommendations should be part, 'Here's what we could get started with right now,' to get some momentum, and part, 'Here's what we need to be working on for a more comprehensive plan going forward.' This is a new focus for us and one where the solutions aren't obvious, so I want to make sure we look broadly at all our options and make sure they're likely to help our students before we implement anything major. But I also know the school board is going to want to see some concrete steps forward."

Leaders face no shortage of problems, which are identified by external sources, stakeholders, and the leaders themselves. And when you look to evidence for help with one problem, your goals or your understanding of the status quo can change, revealing still more problems. We leave it to you to prioritize your problems; our job is to show you how you can use evidence to help solve them.

We'll see how our case-study leaders move through this process. Rebecca Sisti is eager to address the question of what her team can do about chronic absenteeism, but to answer it, she knows she needs to figure out why it is so high now. Maria Gonzalez, the math lead, needs to understand why eighth-grade math scores are so low. And Dwayne Taylor, the state chief, must determine how big of a problem teacher shortages really are for his rural districts.

So that you can work through the thought process alongside these leaders, we'll now ask you to think of one real problem you want to solve. Doing so will help you follow the ideas throughout this book more concretely and work through the steps of evidence use. Don't get bogged down by choosing the biggest or most important problem. Do you have an area in which you're falling short of where you'd like to be—graduation rates, Advanced Placement enrollment, student discipline, differentiated instruction, staffing turnover? If so, you have a problem.[3] We'll get more specific as we go, but we'll start by limiting the problem statement to a single sentence.

Rebecca's sentence is succinct: "We need to lower chronic absenteeism."

Maria writes her sentence: "We need to make sure that students are prepared to perform well on the eighth-grade math assessment."

Dwayne cheats a bit and uses a dash to write his problem in one sentence instead of two: "Rural superintendents need more teachers—could be worse for some certifications."

Diagnose the Problem

The idea of determining the root causes of a problem as a path to solving it seems like the embodiment of common sense. While we love the idea of nailing down root causes, it's hard to do in practice. We consistently see one particular type of problem in root cause analyses: they often identify concerns like low third-grade reading scores as root causes, when these issues are actually educational *outcomes*, not causes. These analyses also frequently assert that a certain factor *causes* an outcome without enough credible evidence to make that claim (much more on this in chapter 3). Finally, the analyses focus so much on factors that schools cannot influence (e.g., student demographics) that they pay insufficient attention to issues that schools and systems can influence (e.g., instructional practice, curriculum, and operations). This last feature of root-cause analyses is particularly concerning because of its implications for equity. It teeters dangerously close to blaming students (or their families or neighborhoods) for their problems and doesn't push hard enough on uncovering the systemic issues within schools that are preventing students from having equitable access to resources and opportunities.

Of course, to address a problem, education leaders must figure out what's driving it, but the term *root cause* has become so distorted in its meaning that we don't use it. We prefer the concept of diagnosing problems. In both medical and educational contexts, diagnoses are informed by many sources: qualitative observations, quantitative measurements, clinical experience, professional judgment, and a body of research. The diagnosis process involves asking questions to gather information. Diagnoses often are speculative, but they are still our best bet for getting a handle on the problem.

The types of questions people usually ask in root-cause analyses are the same ones we suggest for diagnosing a problem. What we want to know is, why do we have this problem? But to be able to work with data to answer the question, we usually ask more specific questions. We might ask, "Is the problem worse when _____?," where we fill in the blank with some school- or classroom-based practice, or "Is the problem worse for _____?," where we fill in the blank with some defining characteristics of students, classrooms, teachers, or schools. These questions ask if the problem is worse under certain conditions or for certain groups.

To move from a general form of the diagnosis question like the preceding examples to a question that lends itself to a research-based answer, we need to get specific. What is the outcome of interest (such as chronic absenteeism rates by school, math scores by grade, or teacher shortage rates by district and position type) that signals the existence of the problem? And to ask if the problem is worse under some circumstances or for some group of people, we'll need to fill in the blanks.

Identify Data on Outcomes

The information that makes problems bubble up to the level of leadership can take various forms. Rebecca received an email from the state about her schools' chronic absenteeism rates, Maria observed lower math performance on the state assessment for eighth graders than for seventh graders, and Dwayne has heard in person, by email, via conference call, and increasingly on Twitter about the hiring woes of his rural superintendents. Chronic absenteeism rates and math performance measures come out of systematically collected data, which aren't always available.

> Before attempting to learn what is behind the rural districts' teacher shortages, Dwayne wants to know whether the shortages even exist—that is, he wants to confirm that his impressions are accurate. But he is not sure how to measure shortages, because the state doesn't track the number or qualifications of applicants or the number of unfilled positions at the district level. He asks Sandy Kennedy, his data manager, how he might get a better handle on these shortages. Sandy suggests focusing on the share of teachers teaching on certification waivers, since in his state, districts wanting to use a waiver must demonstrate that they could not find a qualified applicant with an appropriate teaching

license. Sandy points out that one shortage area, special education, is often staffed with teachers who are certified, but not in special education, and suggests also looking at how many teachers are teaching outside their license areas.

Once they settle on specific quantifiable measures that exist in their data, Dwayne and Sandy can go from the broad question "How big a problem is hiring for rural districts?" to narrower questions, like "How many emergency-certified teachers per pupil are employed in rural districts and other districts?" or "How many special education teachers per pupil are employed in rural districts and other districts?"

▪ ▪ ▪

Maria knows she has a performance problem in terms of the eighth-grade state math assessment, but she also wants to know if the results on the state test reveal problems in other contexts. Is this a general instructional problem or an issue with one test? She asks other questions to provide a more robust body of evidence: Do student report cards also indicate poorer performance in eighth grade than in seventh? What about the results on the formative assessments the district requires? Are these results consistent over the past few years?

Brainstorm Possible Causes of the Problem

Once you've figured out which data reveal your problem, the next step is coming up with a variety of ways to fill in the blank for "Is the problem worse when _____ (or for _____)?" Each possibility will generate its own question. Your team will have many ideas, some of which may be based on preconceived or outdated notions—but that's okay because you will be checking your data to see if these ideas are accurate. You can also look to outside research (discussed in later chapters) for other possible causes to consider. The goal is to come up with multiple plausible hypotheses to investigate with your data. To combat cognitive biases, keep digging even if the data support your first hypothesis. Problems often have multiple causes.

Erin, whom Rebecca has asked to lead the task force on absenteeism, asks the members to come to the first task force meeting with ideas about why the two elementary schools have such high absenteeism rates and what to do about it. Things don't look great in the district's middle or high schools, either, but Erin thinks the reasons for chronic absenteeism are likely to be sufficiently different for younger students that it makes sense to think about their challenges separately. And at the elementary level, she wants to focus now

> on Hillside and Lemont, where the problem is largest. She starts the meeting by asking members to draw on their own experience to think about what might be driving chronic absenteeism at the schools. She hands out sticky notes and has everyone jot down at least a few ideas, each thought on a separate note. "We'll use these to fill in the blanks," she says. "'Is the problem worse when "blank" happens?' 'Is the problem worse for "blank" group?' And I'll ask Keisha Marks, our data manager, if she can check out some of our ideas."

Maria can frame her problem as why the eighth-grade math scores are lagging the seventh-grade scores. She wants to brainstorm how seventh- and eighth-grade instruction are different. To figure this out, she tries a tool called the *five whys*. This protocol, first used by the Toyota Motor Corporation, helps generate many potential explanations for a problem and is therefore useful for diagnosis.[4] Start by writing down the problem, then ask why this is happening. You might list many causes at the beginning of this exercise; the idea is to get to the bottom of each cause before proceeding to the next. Keep asking why, and don't accept the simplest, most available answer. You are done asking why only when you've come up with a set of causes that, if fixed, would eliminate the problem itself.

It takes Maria some digging and repeatedly asking "How do we know?" with the eighth-grade math team to get answers for five rounds of whys.

1. Why are the eighth graders scoring so low on the year-end math exam? Because they haven't mastered the math content. How does Maria know? She sees their low scores on the state tests.

2. Why aren't they mastering the math content? Because throughout the year, teachers are moving on even when students don't understand. How does Maria know this? She checks formative assessments from throughout the year and sees consistent problems.

3. Why are teachers moving on when students don't understand? Because even though teachers are administering formative assessments as required, they are not reteaching content to students who haven't learned the material. How does Maria know that teachers aren't reteaching? She has asked the teachers, and they've told her.

4. Why aren't teachers reteaching this material, as indicated by formative assessments? Because teachers lack sufficient time to stop and review

previously taught material. How does Maria know about the lack of time? The teachers have told her.

5. Why don't teachers have enough time for reteaching? Because there is no extra room in the eighth-grade pacing calendar for reteaching. How does Maria know? She has checked the pacing calendar.

From these discussions, Maria feels convinced that limited time for reteaching is a valid concern for eighth-grade math. But restructuring the units of study to accommodate more reteaching time is a major investment, and she wants to be certain that she has the whole picture. In talking with a few seventh-grade teachers, she learns that their team has built time into the second half of each curriculum unit, just after a formative assessment, to regroup students and reteach the content the children didn't learn the first time. She continues to push on alternative explanations, asking herself, "Could it be the class size? Is the student population the same? Or the experience level of the teachers? Or the curriculum?" She reviews the data, and none of these factors vary across the seventh and eighth grades. The reteaching strategy—the only difference she finds between seventh and eighth grades—seems likely to have caused the difference in performance on the state test.

Maria has gathered much objective information about what the seventh- and eighth-grade teams do differently and similarly. Just because she got this information from talking with her teachers, rather than digging through a database or reading an academic journal, doesn't make it less useful. Indeed, these facts are critical parts of the body of information she needs to review, and it's hard to know how else she could have obtained this information. The important thing when using nonresearch sources of information is to ask how your team knows that the information is correct, rather than just relying on impressions or instincts.

Focus on Actionable Diagnoses

To find out which group of students is most affected by a problem, educators often compare outcomes by student characteristics, such as the student subgroups included on school accountability reports. Schools need to document gaps among subgroups to monitor progress on improving equity. But because a big part of these gaps is determined by factors outside the control of any school system, looking at data only by these subgroups can obscure the school system's role in the problem.

Asking *when* the problem is worse will help move beyond these subgroup analyses, because it focuses attention on access to opportunities that schools provide. Inequitable access to school-based resources and strategies leads to inequitable outcomes. You may not be able to do much about the current and historical policies and social attitudes that systemically harm some of your students outside the school day—but you *can* do something about what happens to them at school. To make progress on equity, start by asking questions about who has access to which opportunities at school.

> Erin divides the whiteboard into sections for student, classroom, school, family, and community factors that could contribute to chronic absenteeism. She asks the task force members to place their sticky notes in whatever section seems the most relevant. After the participants have posted their notes, she points to the *Classroom* and *School* sections of the board. On these sections, several people have stuck ideas marked with observations like "Unwelcoming climate," "Lack of relationships between students and adults at school," "Bullying," and "Transportation." Erin tells the group, "We have no excuses for the part of chronic absenteeism that we're causing ourselves."
>
> By far the most common notation on the tags is "Poverty." Most people have placed their "Poverty" tags in the *Family* and *Community* parts of the board. These two sections also have notes reading "Residential and school mobility" and "Homelessness." Erin points out how many duplicate notes there are in the group. "I wish we could work on partnerships for a big wraparound type of initiative to meet all the needs that come with poverty," she says, "but this year, we can't even begin to think about such a program. So let's focus on the school-based factors more within our control as we think about some small first steps we can take relatively soon. But I don't want to lose all these good ideas, so I'm writing them down for our longer-term investigation and planning."

Maria did an excellent job focusing on actionable diagnoses during her five-whys exercise. She could have easily answered a question like "Why aren't they mastering the math content?" by focusing on factors outside school or blaming the students. Instead, Maria zoomed in on an instructional issue: teachers are moving on even when students don't understand.

When you do the five-whys protocol or other brainstorming exercises, you're likely to come up with some potential diagnoses that you can't do anything about. Consequently, you should conduct the exercise with a designated facilitator who is on the lookout for this dead end and can redirect the conversation as needed. If you're doing it on your own, the protocol is more challenging, but try to watch out for unproductive answers as you reflect.

> Dwayne can think of many reasons why his rural districts are struggling to hire, and they're all variations on a theme: qualified teachers aren't willing to live in those areas for the compensation being offered. When Dwayne thinks about how to fill in the blank in the question "Is the problem worse when ___?" he has lots of ideas. When teachers are paid less? When local labor markets have fewer opportunities for spousal employment? When there are fewer cultural and commercial attractions? These potential causes of the shortage of qualified teachers resonate with what he hears around the state, but he doesn't see how the solutions are within his power.
>
> But some causes depend on state-level decisions. And even if these decisions are up to the legislature or leaders in higher education, Dwayne can still advocate to address these causes. Is the problem worse when the state university system is producing fewer students with the necessary teaching credentials? Is the problem worse when teachers from other states have difficulty transferring their credentials? He asks his data manager Sandy to winnow the list of questions to focus on actionable diagnoses that their team can investigate with existing data and research—and if necessary, to start a new list of additional data they may need to gather.

Rule Out Alternative Explanations

Although it's usually impossible to prove that a factor caused the outcomes you observed, you can often rule out some explanations. For example, the absenteeism task force in the Lincoln School District hypothesized that transportation challenges might be keeping some students from attending school. The group could ask Keisha, the data manager, to check this theory out. She could see whether students who rode the bus were absent more or less frequently than those who walked to school or were driven by their parents. If she found no difference in attendance rates between those three groups, then it would be unlikely that transportation problems were a major contributor to absenteeism.

Ruling out some explanations can help you direct your attention to other possible causes. To frame this step as a "How do I know?" question, ask yourself, "How do I know that what I think is causing the problem is actually causing it? How do I know if some other conditions aren't responsible?" It is perfectly fine, and honest, to conclude, "I don't know for sure, but for all these reasons (fill in with what you've found in the evidence), the hypothesized cause seems pretty likely."

EXAMINE CURRENT AND POTENTIAL STRATEGIES

Questions about a diagnosis are all about your *problem*. The other two main types of questions concern the *strategies* you consider to solve the problem. These questions apply both to potential new strategies and to strategies already in place. For a new strategy, you'll want to consider how others have fared with it. Under what conditions have they implemented it well, and has it improved the outcome of interest to you?

The Every Student Succeeds Act (ESSA) applies the term *evidence-based* to "an activity, strategy, or intervention."[5] Yet many lists or databases of evidence focus on educational products or programs: things you buy from a vendor. Consider this discussion a friendly reminder to ask questions about strategies as we define them, including the full range of activities, interventions, programs, and practices intended to improve student outcomes—not just services offered by vendors. For example, while the way you set your master schedule might not jump to mind as a strategy, it determines which students are assigned to which teachers—and it has big implications for resource equity.

We recommend actively considering multiple strategies, not just the one that is already in place or that has risen to the top in planning discussions. What matters isn't how good any one option is in an absolute sense; it's how good it is compared with the alternatives—including the status quo. In chapter 2, we discuss how to discover what alternatives are available.

Also, don't rush this process. Dwayne needs to spend more time diagnosing his problem before he even knows which strategies he wants to learn more about. If he thinks teachers are leaving the profession for better-paid occupations, then he might want to learn more about tuition forgiveness programs or ways to increase salaries in subject departments and geographic areas that have teacher shortages. But if not enough qualified teachers live in the state to begin with, he may want to investigate options like establishing reciprocal certification with other states or building a pipeline for paraprofessionals to become teachers. He won't be asking any questions about strategies just yet; we'll tackle that issue later in the book.

Assess the Strategy's Implementation

Education research is rife with examples of strategies that apparently failed but that, on closer examination, simply weren't implemented fully or appropriately. For example, researchers compared the effects of different math textbooks on student achievement and found strikingly little difference.[6] The different books all appeared to produce the same results—but most teachers didn't rely on the textbook to guide essential classroom activities, so we would not expect the textbook to make much difference. The answer to "How do I know this strategy would help?" is only useful if you've already come up with a convincing answer to "How do I know we can implement this strategy successfully?" And if you want to evaluate the impact of a strategy already in place, you'll want to assess whether it is being implemented as planned.

When considering a potential new strategy, the broad version of an implementation question is, "How would our implementation of this strategy compare with the best-case scenario?" That is, how would implementation in our district compare with a (near) perfect implementation, done wherever the strategy was originally evaluated? To assess a strategy already in place, we instead ask, "How does our execution of the strategy compare with the best-case scenario?" In either case, the broader question encompasses many narrower ones.

Start with the Best-Case Scenario of Implementation

To understand everything that is needed to implement the strategy well, get specific with who, what, when, where, and how:

- *Who* is supposed to implement the activities that are part of the strategy: teachers, specialists, paraprofessionals, volunteers? How many of these adults are allotted to how many students? How much training will the adults receive, and who will provide it? How would or do the participants feel about this strategy? What barriers would or do they face in implementing it, and how could the participants be helped? How would or do they adapt the strategy from the original concept, initially and over time, consciously and unconsciously?

- *What* activities should take place as part of the strategy? What materials do they require?

- *When* should these activities occur—at what point in the year and in the school day? How often are these activities of the strategy supposed to take place, and for how long? For example, three times a year or three times a day? How long will each activity run? One minute? An hour? Will the activities replace other activities?

- *Where* should these activities take place? Does the use of this location displace some other programming?

■ *How* is the strategy supposed to work? Under what circumstances has it been shown effective? For example, if a strategy was designed and evaluated twenty years ago, will it align with current curricular standards?

The best-case scenario is often not feasible. But by considering these questions, you can think through how much wiggle room the best-case implementation scenario allows—how much you can adapt the strategy to real-life circumstances and still deliver the essence of the strategy. For example, if you are supposed to spend twenty minutes three times a week on an intervention, will twice a week be enough? Once a week? What about if a paraprofessional does it instead of a reading specialist? Or a specialist who has read through the materials but who has not attended the vendor's training?

Identify All the Resources That Implementation Requires

Once you have a better sense of all the activities the strategy involves, you can begin to think about *all* the resources required by the strategy—either the full-on best-case scenario version or whatever scaled-down version you think would still be worth doing. Consider space, scheduling, training, materials, budget, and communications. How much do all the resources cost?

There's no substitute for your knowledge and for much digging to make a list of everything you think is needed to implement the strategy, then pricing out each element. Even when you are considering a strategy involving purchasing something from a vendor, consider the costs beyond the sticker price. You will probably need to acquire more information about the strategy to understand these costs. For example, you'll need to know how much professional development time is needed for implementation, so that you can incorporate the cost of substitute teachers for any professional development during the students' instructional time. A free online tool, CostOut, helps you figure all the costs of executing a strategy and is available from Teachers College at Columbia University.[7]

In calculating your resource needs, you want to consider not just accounting costs (things that show up as budget outlays and therefore come to mind naturally when thinking of costs) but also opportunity costs—everything that doesn't happen because of the activity. If a principal spends two hours coaching, that means he or she can't spend that time doing something else. Maybe someone else can be hired to pick up the slack; if so, the economic cost of having the principal doing the coaching is whatever the district spends on the outsourcing of that other work.

If the principal's original work is not outsourced, then the two hours are probably coming out of the principal's sleep. The dollar value of that time (in salary) should count as an economic cost, even if it is being "donated" by the principal.

Challenges like scheduling problems, space constraints, limited transportation options, and internet bandwidth may make implementing certain strategies a nonstarter, even if costs are reasonable (see the sidebar "Implementation Cost and Feasibility Checklist"). Evaluate your need for resources as precisely as you can up front: if you can't meet key implementation requirements, it doesn't matter how convincing the rest of the evidence is.

Implementation Cost and Feasibility Checklist

To understand the complete set of implementation requirements and associated costs, consider each of the following components for a potential strategy:

- ☐ *Direct costs*: What do you need to pay the vendor or staff directly delivering the strategy?

- ☐ *Time*: How much time do you need, and when do you need it, for training staff in advance, for implementing the strategy, and for collecting related data?

- ☐ *Space*: Do you have the space needed for student groupings? To accommodate the necessary technology? To conduct the necessary training? Is the space available at the same time that the people are available, for all the activities?

- ☐ *Staffing*: Can you afford and find the talent you need? If the stategy is internally staffed, who will cover the staff's other duties, or which activities will the staff be released from to make time for the strategy?

- ☐ *Training*: Who will conduct the training, and at what cost? Who will participate? For how many hours or days, and when will it be scheduled? Where will it be conducted? Are any special materials needed? Will the training take place during time already designated for professional development, or will you need additional substitute coverage or teacher compensation?

- ☐ *Hardware*: What equipment is required? Consider not just computers and tablets, but everything else: headphones, extension cords, power outlets, and so on.

- ☐ *Internet access*: Does the strategy require any specific internet bandwidth? Is there internet access in the space where the strategy will be implemented?

☐ *Scale*: Can you and any vendor implement the strategy at the scale you need? Might you need to stagger implementation over several months or years to reach everyone?

☐ *Funding sources*: Which funds can you use to support this purchase?

As you budget, ask how you know which activities federal and state grants can support. Misperceptions run rampant. Melissa Junge and Sheara Krvaric, attorneys and founding partners of Federal Education Group, encourage districts to review the federal rules themselves, rather than relying on their states or the "compliance industry" to translate the rules. This do-it-yourself approach can pay off. For example, Junge and Krvaric describe their work with a "district official who learned she could use Title I funds for school counselors from reading ED [US Department of Education] guidance, an option her state did not know about. When she showed ED's guidance to her state, they allowed her district to spend on counselors."[8] Once you invest the time to get familiar with these rules, your understanding will open up more flexibility in how federal funds can support your work.

Maria decides she wants to spread the reteaching strategies from the seventh-grade math teachers to the eighth-grade team. Eighth-grade teachers already administer formative assessments in the second half of each unit of study, but now they will use the results to plan a reteaching day that places students in groups according to which strategies the students haven't yet mastered. From her earlier conversations, Maria knows that the biggest barrier the team faces is lack of time. She doesn't anticipate major training needs but realizes she at least needs to figure out what guidance she'll give teachers about the reteaching. If they are to find time for reteaching, she knows they'll need to eliminate or shorten some lessons. She reviews the content on the last three state math exams to determine the extent to which different standards are addressed. Her analysis helps the math team revise the units of study to make room for this new strategy.

Choose Process Measures to Monitor

When you are planning to implement a strategy or evaluate one already under way, the question is, How does or will the implementation of the strategy compare with the best-case scenario? This question requires implementation data, often referred to as *process measures*. Monitoring process measures helps you see if you are on track, as long as the measures are specific and linked to a timeline and (less obvious than you might think) as long as you can obtain the data you need.[9] For example, Maria would need to know what date the assessments are administered, when the teachers will analyze the results, and when the reteaching day will take place. She also could ask the team to write up how they use the results to place the students in groups and how the content was retaught to those groups.

> During a task force meeting that Rebecca Sisti has set up at the Lincoln School District to address absenteeism, Amy Whyte, the principal at Lemont, starts talking about a video she has seen on Facebook. It showed a teacher greeting her students at the classroom door with a high five. Amy thought this practice could be a way of improving school climate and building relationships, and she wonders if it might help with attendance.
>
> Dennis Bollinger, the principal of Hillside, gets excited. "We did this at our school last year! A few of our teachers had seen the video too, and informally it just kind of took hold. People really liked it."
>
> Erin suggests that they look to Hillside's data to see if the high-five greeting has had any impact on attendance. She then asks Dennis how many teachers did it and how consistently—but he doesn't really know. If he had wanted to track this, he could have asked the teachers to report in. Or he could have walked the hallways during greeting time and collected data on what was (and wasn't) happening. Asking teachers to report is likely to be perceived as friendlier, but doing so also means the data are subject to potential problems. For example, the teachers might feel they must say that they've implemented the greeting, or they might not remember what they did. The hallways observations are probably more objective but might be perceived as threatening. When gathering data like these, you'll need to use your best judgment about what your staff will accept and what method will likely produce the most useful information.

Evaluate the Strategy's Impact

The bulk of published research in education—and most evidence aggregators like the What Works Clearinghouse—focuses on evaluating impact. (EdReports is a notable exception: it does not consistently include impact in its reviews of educational products but does assess ease of implementation.) Because of this focus, you'll have more luck looking to existing research on impact questions. As you do, keep in mind that evidence about a strategy's impact reflects how it was implemented under one set of circumstances. These evaluations often involve implementation closer to the best-case scenario than is likely to emerge in practice.

In terms of impact, the big question takes a general form: "How might or did the strategy change outcomes for us?" Again, it's easier to use evidence when you break the broad question into narrower ones (see the sidebar "Examples of Broad and Narrow Evaluation Questions").

Examples of Broad and Narrow Evaluation Questions

BROAD QUESTION	NARROWER QUESTIONS
Rebecca Sisti	
Do individual greetings reduce chronic absenteeism?	How have individual greetings affected chronic absenteeism elsewhere? Attendance? What factors might affect attendance? How did chronic absenteeism change at Hillside when individual greetings were implemented there last year?
Maria Gonzalez	
Does reteaching affect eighth-grade math performance?	How do this year's eighth graders (with reteaching) fare compared with last year? What does the existing research say about reteaching in general? For math? For middle school?
Dwayne Taylor	
What policies are promising for improving rural teacher recruitment and retention?	Would establishing reciprocal certification with other states be cost-effective? How much impact might that have? What impact would state-funded tuition forgiveness have? How would tuition forgiveness compare with the state's supplying funds for districts to supplement salaries?

Because the existing research base plays a larger role in questions of impact than in issues of diagnosis or implementation, the upcoming chapters will focus on impact questions. In chapter 2, we explain how to find the existing research, and in chapter 3, how to determine if it is relevant and convincing. In chapter 3, we examine how to assess the quality and match of quantitative research. In both chapters 2 and 3, the lessons will apply disproportionately to questions of impact. In chapter 4, we map the characteristics of impact studies to ESSA's levels of evidence.

KEY TAKEAWAYS

* Research is structured to answer specific questions, so turn your problem into questions.

* Most questions about problems and how to solve them fall into three types:

  * Questions that *diagnose* the problem

  * Questions that *assess the implementation* of a strategy and help with feasibility and cost

  * Questions that *evaluate the impact* of a strategy on the problem

* Turn a broad question into many narrower questions to increase the odds of finding objective answers. These techniques can help:

  * Ask, "How do I know (something I think is true is true)?"

  * Ask the five whys.

  * Ask questions about many possible explanations, not just the one you have immediately in mind.

APPLY YOUR LEARNING

☐ Write a one-sentence statement of your problem.

☐ Where would you find outcomes data to use for diagnosing the problem? Be specific about how you will measure the outcome: for individual students or aggregated into classrooms, schools, or another grouping? When will you measure the outcome, and for whom?

☐ Make a list of endings to both these questions:

  * "Is the problem worse when _____?" Fill in the blank to assess how the problem relates to access to school-based resources or strategies.

  * "Is the problem worse for _____?" Fill in the blank with characteristics of students, teachers, classrooms, schools, and so forth.

☐ Choose one (probably speculative) diagnosis from the list that relates to a school-based resource or strategy you can influence. What data could you use to answer the question?

☐ Try the five whys with the diagnosis question you picked. For each answer, ask yourself, "How do I know?"

☐ Use what you've learned from the five whys to write down at least two potential strategies for improving the problem. Be creative.

☐ Choose one of those two potential strategies, or pick a strategy you are currently using. Describe the ideal implementation of the strategy with as much detail as possible. What resources does it require? How do they compare to your capacity? How would you know that implementation is going well or why it's off track if it isn't going well? What would you measure to monitor implementation progress?

2

KNOW WHERE TO FIND
USEFUL RESEARCH FAST

With your questions in hand, now is the time to start looking for research to inform the answers. Here, we'll focus on research that was conducted by others—so it already exists. You can find it in various places, including books, academic journals, reports from government agencies or advocacy groups, blog posts, and other education journalism. In this chapter, we'll show you how to look for research to answer your questions and how to understand the incentives and perspectives of the many information providers out there. In chapter 3, we'll turn to how to critically assess the research findings. Practitioners consistently tell us that time is a huge barrier to using evidence, so throughout this discussion, we'll show you how to get the lay of the land quickly and make the most of however much time you have.

WHERE TO GET THE BIG PICTURE

If you remember one thing from this chapter, it should be this: *if you can avoid it, don't base a decision solely on a single study.* Survey data consistently reveal that education leaders do not read original research studies, such as those published in academic journals, so this advice may sound like an easy lift. The challenge is that many sources that leaders do rely on in their decision-making—sources like websites that rate educational products and endorse strategies, advocacy reports, and educational journalism—themselves often report on a single study. These sources often frame their pieces in general ways: readers could misinterpret a summary of a single new study as a bottom-line review of the relevant body of research. In this chapter, we first explain why one study is not enough and why the big picture is better. Then we'll turn to how to find overviews you can trust.

Pitfalls of Using Only One Study

In 2013, medical researchers Jonathan Schoenfeld and John Ioannidis published a review of the research literature on whether eating any of fifty common foods is related to cancer.[1] They found that studies often yielded wildly different results for the same food—some seeming to show that the food caused cancer, others that the food prevented it. But any one of these studies on its own might seem conclusive in its findings. If you come across a newspaper article describing a new study that found eating beef is associated with a lower risk of cancer, you could come away from the article ready to order up your favorite burger.

How can studies published by honest researchers reach contrary findings? First, the studies often rely on different information. They may collect data from different types of people, over different periods, asking participants for different information. In chapter 3, we'll explain how to read studies closely to notice these distinctions and how seemingly similar studies may actually be answering different questions.

Second, even when researchers intentionally make the same choices as in previous studies, they are often unable to replicate those findings. This happens so frequently that it's known as the *replication crisis*. Researchers, like anyone else, subconsciously can anticipate that their research will yield findings consistent with their already-established beliefs. If the results conflict with those expectations, the investigators may question the research strategy, rather than what it reveals, and subtly tinker with the strategy. If different researchers have different beliefs, they'll tinker in different ways—and readers may not be able to observe these differences.

These subtle biases can even affect researchers who are trying hard to be objective in their search for answers. Researchers are coming to terms with their cognitive biases and are adjusting their research methods to guard against these problems. One promising approach is requiring researchers to preregister a study. The investigators must commit to key elements of their research design before receiving access to the data and, consequently, before seeing any results.

People sometimes talk about the peer review process used by some academic journals as if it guarantees the quality and accuracy of a published paper. Peer review adds value by having additional, neutral researchers weigh in on a study, but it doesn't deliver an absolute judgment of whether a result is accurate. Peer reviewers do not attempt to replicate findings, check statistical analyses for errors, or examine data sources, and peer-reviewed work can contain errors. Finally, what's insufficient for one peer-reviewed journal is often good enough for a different peer-reviewed journal.

Luckily, for many topics, enough studies have been conducted that a big picture usually emerges, despite the potential weaknesses of any individual study. The body of information is much richer than a single piece of information.

Systematic Reviews for the Big Picture

To enjoy the benefits of research while minimizing the risk of getting bad information from a single study, focus on the big picture. Look for overviews, ideally pieces reviewing the literature systematically (that is, including all studies meeting explicit search criteria) rather than highlighting a few handpicked studies.

We recommend starting your search with two sources for systematic reviews: the Campbell Collaboration (campbellcollaboration.org) and the What Works Clearinghouse (https://ies.ed.gov/ncee/wwc). The Campbell Collaboration describes itself as "an international social sciences research network that produces high-quality, open and policy-relevant evidence syntheses, plain language summaries and policy briefs." In 2019, the Campbell Collaboration had forty-one reviews on different topics in education. Topics included those that frequently arise in debates about US policy and practice: for example, class size, school discipline, year-round schooling, and school start times. Other reviews included syntheses of evidence on models like the Tools of the Mind curriculum and no excuses charter schools. For most topics, the reviews (which can exceed one hundred pages) are accompanied by two-page plain-language summaries.

The WWC is a federal effort to share information about "what works" in education, with transparent review requirements and processes to eliminate conflicts of interest. The clearinghouse was established before ESSA, and its review standards are quite technically rigorous: many studies that meet ESSA's requirements are ineligible for WWC review. The WWC content is more complex to navigate than that of the Campbell Collaboration (see the sidebar "Navigating the What Works Clearinghouse" for tips). We find the WWC's "Practice Guides" and "Intervention Reports" to be its most useful products.

Navigating the What Works Clearinghouse

The WWC offers quick links on the home page with three ways to search for evidence. Here's how to choose your starting point.

INTERVENTION REPORTS (SYSTEMATIC REVIEWS)

What the WWC calls "interventions" are (generally) proprietary strategies and products—in other words, things vendors sell. Because the clearinghouse reviews the body of available research, you can find one review that spans multiple research studies on the same intervention.

Search the "Intervention Reports" link when you are considering a proprietary intervention and want information on its track record. The WWC's review standards assess the quality and relevance of the data to the particular topic, the strength of the evidence that an intervention is effective, and the consistency of the findings across studies. Just keep in mind that the WWC standards for which studies are eligible for review exclude some that would count as evidence under some of ESSA's definitions (we'll discuss this in more depth later).

PRACTICE GUIDES

The Practice Guides make research-based recommendations educators can implement without buying specific proprietary materials. Again, the clearinghouse reviews the body of available research, so you can look to one review that spans multiple studies. The guides are organized by content and grade span. For example, there are reviews titled "Improving Mathematical Problem Solving in Grades 4 Through 8" and "Teaching Elementary School Students to Be Effective Writers." The practice guides include documents linking research citations to each recommendation. For some topics, recommendations are informed by "supplemental" studies that do not meet WWC group design standards but may meet ESSA standards. Use the practice guides for the following objectives:

- to figure out what to do, rather than what to buy
- to synthesize best practices for a particular grade level and content area, including materials designed for practitioners
- to incorporate a broader view of evidence than the WWC standards applied to the reviews of individual studies

REVIEWS OF INDIVIDUAL STUDIES

Individual studies assess the effect of one intervention on a particular group. WWC reviews individual studies and rates them according to the quality of evidence and study

design. Each review in the WWC contains information on the study design; the characteristics of the study's sample, including the size and grade range; and a summary of the
findings. Search reviews of individual studies for the following objectives:

- ■ to search for studies reviewed by the WWC in a particular topic area
- ■ to see if a particular study has been reviewed by the WWC
- ■ to learn more about an individual study or its rating

Systematic reviews are excellent tools for understanding the impact of defined
strategies. They are generally less useful when it comes to diagnosing problems or
uncovering implementation requirements and challenges. Plus, many topics aren't
covered in such reviews.

> Erin Frazier, the counselor at Lemont in charge of leading the task force for the Lincoln
> School District, looks up attendance and chronic absenteeism in the Campbell Collabo-
> ration and the WWC. Unfortunately, nothing posted there seems to apply to her ques-
> tions about elementary schools.[2]

■   ■   ■

> Meanwhile, in another school district, Maria Gonzalez wants to know what strategies
> for formative assessment and reteaching have worked the best for middle school math
> students. First, she visits the WWC and filters her searches for mathematics. She looks
> at the "Grades Examined" column and clicks on the first item, the Knowledge Is Power
> Program. She reads the first page of the intervention report, realizes that it is a charter
> school network based on a comprehensive school model, and quickly presses the "Back"
> button. Knowing that she doesn't have money in her budget to invest in a program, she
> ignores the programs with a trademark symbol. She clicks on two other interventions
> but quickly sees that they are unrelated to the formative assessment and reteaching
> approach that she is trying to implement.
>
> She then tries the "Practice Guides" section, which has much more content related
> to strategies that don't require buying branded products. She's briefly waylaid by a
> report on strategies for improving mathematical problem solving in fourth to eighth
> grade. It looks useful, but it is not about formative assessment. She makes a note to
> return to it another time and to tell her colleagues in other subjects to check out the
> practice guides. After ten minutes on the site, she gives up. What now? she wonders.

Risks of Less Systematic Reviews

When you struggle to find a systematic review of research in the area you want to examine (which is, to be fair, much of the time), it's time to look for something less systematic. This means searching for evidence in the same way you would look for anything else on the internet, whether with a search engine or through a trusted source like *Education Week* (you can access three free articles per month even without a subscription). If you use a search engine here, make it a standard one, not an academic one (e.g., Google, not Google Scholar), because you're looking for a recent nonacademic overview piece that speaks to practical concerns.

> Erin prepared for the first meeting of the chronic absenteeism task force by spending her lunch hour online. She started with searching for "attendance" and "absence," and found it helpful to add the word "school." She found that the results were even more focused when she tried the more specific term "chronic absenteeism." She narrowed the search to elementary schools by adding "elementary" and then added "-middle" to yield results focused only on elementary schools. There are tradeoffs between broader searches, which return more hits, and narrower ones, which could inadvertently miss something useful. Every search is different, so rather than offering hard-and-fast rules for how to search, we recommend experimenting with a few sets of terms before you narrow down your results.
>
> Searching the whole internet yielded so many results that Erin decided to search from the *Education Week* site instead. There, she found a blog on how schools could reduce absences.[3] The post summarized findings from "Attendance Playbook: Smart Solutions for Reducing Chronic Absenteeism."[4]

Sometimes these searches will lead you to accessible, open-source overviews from places that seem objective. If you don't find a current, topical report like this, expand your search to look for an academic overview before you resort to studies of individual strategies.

Academic overviews typically come in one of three forms: stand-alone literature reviews, literature reviews found within a single study on that topic, and meta-analyses. Literature reviews describe quantitative and qualitative research, explaining areas of agreement or disagreement. Meta-analyses synthesize the numeric results from quantitative studies. *Journalist's Resource* has a tip sheet for finding literature reviews and meta-analyses.[5]

Both types of research syntheses—literature reviews and meta-analyses—should describe their criteria for including individual studies. Read these criteria to understand what answers count for the review. In chapter 3, we'll talk about what makes individual studies relevant and convincing. For now, we'll leave it at "garbage in, garbage out." A synthesis that turns multiple unconvincing or irrelevant findings into one single number or rating will not magically eliminate the flaws of what went into it.

You can find short literature reviews within most academic journal articles (the single studies we warn you about using in isolation); authors typically show how their research builds on existing knowledge. At the very least, these articles will cite references on their topic, which can be helpful. Good research cites both the research that supports the authors' findings and the research that suggests otherwise. Almost every topic has studies that fall into both categories, so be suspicious if the discussion of the literature seems one-sided. It's worth looking at the most recent studies available, even if they are not precisely on your topic of interest, for the literature review alone.

Within any overview, you're likely to find a couple of paragraphs describing the research findings most applicable to your situation. You should read these closely. For findings you may act on, look for evidence to back up the assertions underlying these findings, either in the overview (check links and footnotes too) or in the original study it describes. Citations often lead to older assertions, rather than facts to prove the findings. Don't assume that there's a fact at the foundation; it might just be a house of cards.

HOW TO FIND ACADEMIC SOURCES

As we've discussed, academic sources typically aren't our first choice, but sometimes you will want to use them. But identifying and obtaining them is easier said than done. It can be particularly important to find the full text of a study when something you read might meaningfully influence your actions. As Rachael Gabriel, professor of literacy education at the University of Connecticut, says, "Precision, context, and evidence often go missing in the long game of telephone that reaches from the findings of researchers to the eyes of most readers."[6] To find enough information to judge how relevant and convincing a claim is, you sometimes need to track down citations and get the original study in hand.

For academic searches, we highly recommend Google Scholar (scholar.google.com), which has no close competitor for free searches for research in terms of what it catalogs and its search functionality (see the sidebar "How to Use Google

Scholar"). ERIC (eric.ed.gov), sponsored by the US Department of Education, indexes citations and often includes full-text versions of education research. Google Scholar may bring you to ERIC for a pdf of an article.

How to Use Google Scholar

Searching for "chronic absenteeism" on Google Scholar returned about ninety-six thousand results (in the middle of 2019). You can narrow your searches by publication date or by adding more search terms. Google Scholar has a page of helpful search tips.*

Each citation is followed by an excerpt of the paper's abstract, to give the viewer a quick peek into the paper. Clicking on the title brings you to the full text of the abstract, even if the full study is behind a paywall. The bottom line of each Google Scholar entry includes how to find related studies and the full text of the study at hand:

- "Cited by . . . " takes you to all (necessarily more recent) studies citing the current study. This link is especially useful when you are starting with an older study and want to know the latest thinking on the topic. More heavily cited studies are not necessarily more methodologically sound, but they may have greater influence on people's beliefs.
- "Related articles" takes you to just that: related articles. Google does not describe the algorithm it uses to determine which articles are related.
- "All *x* versions" takes you to all the places on the internet that Google Scholar can find the study in its entirety. This link is useful when some sources are available by subscription only; you may find a free (sometimes identified as "ungated") version posted on a personal website or in a repository of prepublication working papers.

*Google Scholar, "Search Tips," https://scholar.google.com/intl/en/scholar/help.html.

Maria turns to Google Scholar for help. She uses the advanced-search feature (which she finds by clicking on the (very subtle) menu link in the upper left-hand corner) and populates the following fields:

- "With all of the words": mathematics
- "With at least one of the words": assessment reteaching differentiation quiz grouping targeted formative interim

The top hit is a study titled "From Testing to Teaching: The Use of Interim Assessment in Classroom Instruction"—and she is relieved to see it links directly to the paper rather than a journal article behind a paywall.[7] Maria reads the abstract and decides that the full article is worth reading more closely. With her weekly department meeting about to begin, she blocks off twenty minutes of her schedule for the following day. While she feels guilty that she will be spending a little less time observing classrooms that week, she knows that dedicating time to understand the research will make the teachers more effective in the long run.

Academic journals typically are available by subscription only, but if you are just looking for an article or two, you can often find a way around the paywalls. The sidebar "How to Access Research Without Paying?" gives some helpful hints for working around this digital barrier.

How to Access Research Without Paying?

When the study you want requires a subscription, you can try a few things to get to the gist of an article without having to subscribe.

- *Try the abstract of the paper.* The abstract is usually available for free even when the full text of the paper is not, and this summary may have all the details you need. It is also short (usually less than two hundred words) and is generally more thoughtfully written and edited than the rest of the paper. Professional researchers read many more abstracts than they read papers.
- *Check the academic website of each author.* Authors often post preprint versions of publications that may not have the same formatting as the journal version has, but the posts typically have the same content—and are available for free.
- *Use Google Scholar to search for the article.* You may find a version of the paper that was posted for a presentation or as a reading assignment for a course. You may also find it through a working paper series like EdWorkingPapers.com or through ERIC; these versions would appear in the Google Scholar search results.
- *In a pinch, email the authors directly.* A quick Google search will usually turn up the author's professional email address, particularly for researchers based at universities and larger research firms. You'll probably be surprised at how glad they will be to facilitate someone's reading their work.

WHO'S ON FIRST? PLAYERS IN THE EVIDENCE GAME

Whether research makes its way to you in a headline, a tweet, a report, a blog post, or some clearinghouse, whatever you're viewing is a direct result of individual people's choices about what to include and exclude. For this reason, it's helpful to know who those people are. Some individuals and organizations conduct research, some fund it, and others interpret, summarize, rate, or aggregate it. And many parties fill more than one of these roles simultaneously. For example, one person can be an academic researcher, a contractor to research organizations, a vendor, and a writer for media outlets.

In this section, we discuss common sources of research: professional associations, media coverage, advocacy groups, think tanks, vendors, and organizations we call evidence translators and evidence aggregators. All these groups share research findings in some form, whether the findings are in their original form or are translated, summarized, stripped down, or aggregated up. This section gives a quick overview of the types of players you'll encounter in this constantly changing landscape. It suggests where to find evidence and how to evaluate sources yourself. If you rely on any source often, it's worth the investment to understand not only how it is funded, but also the leanings of any organizations supporting the work.[8]

Professional Associations

In the national survey on research use, the most common way that district respondents reported accessing research "often" or "all the time" was through their professional associations, at 53 percent.[9] Professional associations frequently include researchers as speakers at conferences and on webinars, and some associations include summaries of new research in their periodicals. Just as with any other source, you should check out for yourself any claim or finding you are considering acting on.

Media

Media can be a great way to stay up-to-date on education research and policy. We particularly enjoy *Phi Delta Kappan*, *Education Week* (including their research blog), *Education Next*, and *Chalkbeat* for their accessible and relatively objective coverage of education research. If you're more of a podcast person, try *Educate* or *Education Next*. National Public Radio and its local affiliates cover education news and research. These sources represent a range of viewpoints.

We offer two cautions for consuming education news even from established sources. First, philanthropic sources don't just fund straight-up advocacy—they also fund media, in ways readers may not expect. Find out who is paying for your coverage, and look for conflicts of interest and disclosure policies (tip: you might need to scroll all the way to the end of a piece to see the disclosures at the bottom). You don't need to rule out sources because of this information, but it can help you understand why a source is covering the stories it does and the values of those writing and editing for the media source. Also keep in mind that journalists are always looking for content. This focus gives a leg up to those who send tips and press releases or who host events and issue reports. But it's people and organizations with resources and agendas—including advocates and vendors—that do those things. Even when journalists cover the content objectively and professionally, money still shapes what makes it to the reader.

Advocacy Groups and Think Tanks

Advocacy groups may do their own research or promote others' research, and they provide a wealth of content. It's free, and compared with academic writing or government reports, the content is quite accessible and engaging. They also have policy agendas that reflect the specific interests of their memberships or donors. And the names of these groups, like the Foundation for Excellence in Education or the Education Trust, typically reveal little about these agendas.

Some advocacy groups that conduct research call themselves think tanks. This label is confusing, because think tanks typically describe themselves as independent. But however a group bills itself, unless it has its own large endowment, it needs to raise money from somewhere. To understand the chain of influence, follow the money. The easiest place to start is the organization's own website. It should show who donates to the organization, who leads it, and who sits on its board. Look to these names to get a clearer picture of potential conflicts of interest across organizations. Journalist's Resource offers more tips on investigating think tanks.[10]

> In her search for more information on chronic absenteeism, Erin notes that "Attendance Playbook," which she has found on an *Education Week* blog, was written jointly by FutureEd, a self-described "independent, solution-oriented think tank at Georgetown University's McCourt School of Public Policy," and by Attendance Works, "a national nonprofit initiative that supports improved policy and practices around school attendance."[11] She checks out both sources and notices that Attendance Works provides fee-based consulting services, in addition to sponsoring research and advocacy. But she sees plenty of strategies in the playbook that her team could implement without buying any technical assistance or consulting from Attendance Works. Now, if she were trying to decide

whether to focus on attendance instead of another area, like curriculum or tutoring, she might be a bit suspicious about the materials, given the groups' clear mission of promoting the importance of attendance. But she decides that since she is already prioritizing attendance, and since Attendance Works is endorsing approaches beyond its own products, "Attendance Playbook" is a sufficiently credible source for her needs.

Vendors

Marketing materials pose an obvious red flag as a source of evidence.[12] Unfortunately, it's not always obvious who is a vendor. Vendors may be structured as not-for-profit organizations or university-based centers. But anyone who sells stuff is likely to care about sales. And even when vendors are clearly identified, customers are susceptible to more influence than one might think. When academic medical centers in some states restricted how drug reps could interact with physicians, including banning branded gifts such as notepads and pens with drug names and company logos, the market share of the affected drugs fell by 9 percent.[13]

Some of the evidence vendors produce shows up in academic journals, which provide the affiliations of authors. But just because a researcher holds an academic position does not mean that the researcher is not also a vendor. Most academic journals require authors to reveal any potential conflicts of interest so that the reader can see any affiliations or conflicts, but not all sources translating that research will be so detailed. Conducting a quick internet search on the author is a low-cost way to learn more.

Evidence Translators

Some outlets curate evidence and provide it in accessible formats for practitioners and leaders. These *evidence translators* may describe a single study or the state of the research literature overall. As you'd expect, some translators describe research more accurately and usefully than others do. A few of our (free) favorites are Usable Knowledge, the Scholars Strategy Network, and the Conversation.[14] These sources rely on a highly curated selection of contributions from academic researchers and share the implications of this research for practice and policy. We also recommend following your local Regional Education Laboratory. The US Department of Education's Institute of Education Sciences sponsors ten such laboratories across the country to help people in education agencies and other people use data and research to improve their work.[15] Leaders repeatedly mentioned one particular paid subscription service to us: the *Marshall Memo*, a weekly newsletter covering research and news of interest to education leaders, is well respected for its carefully curated content.

Teachers are uniquely positioned to connect research to the authentic challenges of practice and are increasingly translating research publicly. One example is the rise of the nonprofit researchED. Tom Bennett, the organization's founder and director, describes researchED as "a grass-roots, teacher-led project that aims to make teachers research-literate and pseudo-science proof."[16] In the same way that other sources must be viewed with care, just because a beloved teacher writes with great confidence about what the research shows doesn't mean that the interpretation is correct—or that the findings themselves are convincing and relevant to your situation.

> A few people at the chronic absenteeism team meeting start talking about the viral high-five video. Erin is intrigued, but cautious. "We don't want to ask all our teachers to change their practice and choose this approach over something else," she says, "just because we saw a cute video on Facebook." Dennis Bollinger, the principal of Hillside, cuts in. "Oh, don't worry. It came from Edutopia."

Edutopia is a site run by the George Lucas Educational Foundation.[17] Its popularity, with over a million followers each on Facebook and Twitter, and over a hundred thousand YouTube subscribers, is driven by its actionable content for educators, with high-production-quality videos and blogs.[18] Only some of Edutopia's content is linked to research findings. Much of it is created by teachers describing what they have found useful in their own classrooms, often without the benefit of systematic evaluation. Edutopia can spark creativity, but if you are looking to it as a source for research, check the links. Some refer to other Edutopia posts by researchers, who are synthesizing some part of the literature themselves (though not necessarily with systematic reviews), while others go to Edutopia posts describing practices rather than research findings.

Evidence Aggregators

Many states and associations are directing their agencies and members to what we'll call *evidence aggregators* (e.g., the WWC). These aggregators deliver a highly simplified perspective on research, often rating its strength in some way. The idea of these online resources is appealing: a one-stop shop to learn what strategies are effective. Unsurprisingly, the number of these aggregators has been growing since ESSA ratcheted up the demands for evidence use. Evidence aggregators are explicitly designed to answer only impact evaluation questions, not diagnosis or implementation ones. Rather than answering nuanced questions about the impact of the strategy and the contexts in which similar impacts could be expected, they typically restrict their reporting to the more cut-and-dried, technical aspects. For example, evidence aggregators base their selection of strategies and their ratings on the design of the research studies that evaluate the strategies. Only if the study uses permissible research methods do the aggregators consider whether the strategy had a measured impact. Consequently, the aggregators strip out nuance that could help show how you might fare with the strategy under different local circumstances or if you implement a modified version of it.

These evidence aggregators operate under a range of business models, and the field is changing all the time. Rather than exhaustively cataloging the options—and being out of date by the time a hard copy of this book makes its way into your hands—we suggest you follow the same strategy with aggregators as with other sources: understand who is running the show, who is paying, how transparent they are about the criteria for inclusion and how these criteria are applied, and whether there are any potential conflicts of interest (see the sidebar "Questions for an Evidence Aggregator"). You wouldn't trust the *Consumer Reports* auto issue if Toyota produced it, so before you rely on an aggregator, follow the money.

Speaking of *Consumer Reports*, the popular EdReports.org site describes itself as "a sort of 'Consumer Reports' for school materials."[19] EdReports is taking a teacher-led, demand-driven approach that fills a void in the aggregator market by reviewing curricular materials for content, alignment with current standards, and ease of use. The organization's review teams rely on internally developed rubrics for what constitutes high-quality, implementable, standards-aligned content. They use research as an input into these rubrics, but they do not require research to prove that a product causes an improvement in student outcomes to rate that product highly. In contrast, the WWC explicitly reviews research studies, rather than educational products themselves. A high rating from WWC means that research has provided methodologically rigorous support for a strategy, but the rating says nothing about the strategy's alignment with curricular standards or how easy it is to use.

Evidence aggregators provide information about whether programs and practices were effective in the context in which they were evaluated. They are a tempting solution for administrators who want to comply with murky evidence mandates. But no single resource says whether something is cost-effective, feasible, and a good idea for you.

> **Questions for an Evidence Aggregator**
>
> The education landscape is constantly evolving. It includes the products and strategies to be reviewed, the research used to evaluate them, and the formats for aggregating that research. But you can always use the following basic questions to get to the bottom of what any one-stop shop provides:
>
> - Who funds this resource? Who produces it? For both funder and producer, look for a conflict-of-interest policy and any disclosures. If you don't see such a policy, check to see if any key players are also vendors.
> - Who reviews the products and strategies? How many people review each item? What training do they receive?
> - If information about a product or strategy is delivered in some report-card style, with a categorical rating, a certain number of stars, or a "good enough to be on the recommended list" setup, what do the different ratings mean?
> - Do the ratings capture demonstrated impact on achievement (based on well-designed research); alignment with standards; ease of implementation; or any other quality measures?
> - How does the aggregator decide which products to review? Is there a backlog?
> - For ratings based on research:
>   - Does a low rating or being left off a list mean that a *product* was reviewed and deemed low quality? Or does it mean that the *research methods* used to evaluate the product did not meet the aggregator's criteria?
>   - How many studies are used in reviewing each product or strategy? A review based on a single study shares the same dangers as reading just one study yourself.
>   - Does the aggregator provide information on the studies used, ideally including the dates of the studies, and information about the sample size and setting to help judge relevance?

Philanthropy

Whether you are trying to get a handle on the agenda of an advocacy group, a think tank, an education blog, or an evidence aggregator, at the end of the money trail, you will often find a philanthropic organization. Like the names of their grantees, the names of funders don't tell the whole story. While the different interests of a vendor and a teachers' union are intuitive, it's often harder to discern the motivation of foundations. Secretary of Education Betsy DeVos's high profile means that many readers would expect the Dick and Betsy DeVos Family Foundation to advocate for policies like vouchers and charter schools, but they may be less aware that the Walton Family Foundation supports a similar agenda. And the priorities of some foundations shift over time as they learn more about past successes and failures. To find out more about a foundation, check out its website. Look for the "About Us" or "Mission" links. For more specifics, look for a database of its grants on the website, to see what grantees and activities the foundation supports.

Your Own Expertise and Judgment

Research is just one piece of what many of these groups and individuals do. Though they may have built up your trust over time, trustworthiness is generally different from being a skilled and responsible wielder of research. That's why, when you identify a claim that might influence your actions, there is no substitute for checking it out yourself. You might have to hunt down the original source of evidence if it was not described in enough detail in the overview.

The sidebar "Step-by-Step Guide to Finding the Big Picture" guides you on the sequence of steps both to save time and to obtain a high-level, unbiased overview. The sequence has the added advantage of minimizing the challenges of finding access to journal articles from behind paywalls and parsing their technical language.

Step-by-Step Guide to Finding the Big Picture

1. **Search for a systematic review of the related research.**
   - **Look for these features:** the source explicitly describes the criteria for inclusion in the review and covers all the pieces meeting those criteria. The source should also be recently published or updated.
   - **Look here:** the Campbell Collaboration and the WWC (specifically "Practice Guides" and "Intervention Reports"). Look beyond the ratings, and read the text.

2. **Search for a nonacademic overview of the topic.**
   - **Look for these features:** you can follow the money to understand the potential bias of those funding, conducting, and disseminating the research. The overview should be recently published or updated, should acknowledge (not necessarily

with equal weight) arguments on both sides of an issue, and should provide data or citations for its assertions.

— **Look here:** nonacademic search engines; *Education Week*; bloggers who have earned your trust by consistently backing their claims with research and data.

3. **Search for an academic overview of the topic.**

— **Look for these features:** whether it is a literature review or a meta-analysis, the study should explicitly describe the criteria for inclusion and any exceptions. Those criteria should accord with your view of what is relevant and convincing. The overview should also be recently published and should exclude outdated research studies. If you can't find one of these overview pieces, look for an overview in the literature review or background section of a recent single study on a narrower topic.

— **Look here:** Google Scholar and the Education Resources Information Center (ERIC).

Eric Kalenze is the Minneapolis teacher who brought researchED events to the United States. When we asked him how he reviews submissions for those events, his answer was simple: "I click the links." That is, when authors provide hyperlinks to support their assertions, he actually checks them out. In the next chapter, we explain how to go to the source yourself to judge how relevant and convincing a research finding is for *your* question.

KEY TAKEAWAYS

* Be wary of single studies and, by extension, reports that mainly summarize a single new study.

* Look for overview pieces instead, ideally systematic reviews that transparently report their criteria for inclusion (e.g., the Campbell Collaboration and the What Works Clearinghouse "Practice Guides" and "Intervention Reports").

* When you can't find a systematic review on your topic, turn to other sources for the big picture. Look closely at key assertions. Do the authors back up their points with data or citations? If so, check the citations.

* Acknowledge that everyone who produces or shares evidence faces incentives—some of which may not be aligned to your interests. Follow the money

to find out who you're dealing with, including media and philanthropic organizations.

* Understand what does and doesn't show up in evidence aggregators. If you use an aggregator often, invest some time in understanding its model.

* When you lack other options and are looking for academic research, use Google Scholar to identify what is the most influential and recent.

APPLY YOUR LEARNING

☐ Choose a question you've posed in chapter 1, and experiment with a few sets of search terms. Can you find any overview pieces to give you the big picture?

☐ Skim the overviews you found. Did you find useful information? How are any claims you might rely on supported, and how can you know that they are accurate? Can you track down the original sources?

☐ Who provided the overviews? Can you tell who paid for them? Do the funders hold particular interests or policy positions that might influence the coverage?

☐ Experiment with the Google Scholar tips and different search terms to identify one stand-alone study that might help answer one of your questions. Attempt to find its full text for free.

☐ Think of the last few times you've encountered research findings when you weren't actively searching. What sources did they come from? Check out the sources, and see what you can learn about their mission.

3

DETERMINE HOW RELEVANT AND CONVINCING THE RESEARCH IS

When you find yourself rethinking a strategic plan, contemplating a major initiative, or making a big purchase like a new curriculum, you'll want evidence that your plan, initiative, or curriculum will effectively address the problem you are trying to solve. To this end, the research findings supporting your decision must be relevant to your situation and convincing before you move forward.

In this chapter, we explain what makes research relevant and convincing for answering your own questions. You'll learn how to cut through the jargon to dissect a study, finding the key elements you need. We'll focus here on large-scale, quantitative studies of the impact of strategies on outcomes. These types of studies are just one way to answer a question, and they are often ill suited for help with diagnosing problems or assessing the implementation of strategies. We'll discuss other sources of useful information in the coming chapters.

So, what do we mean by relevant and convincing? The most relevant research sets out to answer questions most like your own; the most convincing research provides highly persuasive answers to whichever questions the researchers pose. The important thing is to focus on how relevant and convincing the studies are, rather than the extent to which they confirm your prior beliefs.

RELEVANT FOR YOU; CONVINCING FOR YOU AND OTHERS

To show what we mean by relevance, we'll consider the plight of two other case-study characters, each considering research on the effects of class-size reduction. Jill Ahmad is the principal of a high-poverty urban high school with forty students in each English class. She is considering cutting some programs to decrease

English class sizes to around thirty students. She has heard that "research shows"—with a randomized control trial, no less!—that smaller class sizes improve student achievement. When she digs into that statement, she learns that it is based on the Tennessee Student Teacher Achievement Ratio study from the 1980s. In this study, class sizes in early elementary grades were lowered from about twenty-two to about fifteen students per class in districts across Tennessee. Jill concludes that the study is irrelevant to her decision. The research doesn't say that class-size reduction is useless, but she still considers its value an open question for her situation. Meanwhile, Krista Chu, an elementary school principal in a better-funded district, is trying to decide how to allocate staff and whether to reduce her class sizes from twenty-four to nineteen students. She finds the same study much more relevant, though she does wonder if changes since the 1980s in things like prekindergarten attendance, the academic focus of early grades, and curricular standards would make the impact of class size different now. As these two examples show, no outside entity can uniformly judge the relevance of research: it all depends on who wants to know.

The idea of objectively rating research quality is a more natural fit with the notion of how convincing a study is—that is, how well the study answers the question its authors ask, rather than how relevant that question is for any reader. In light of the Tennessee study's random assignment of students and teachers to larger and smaller classes, both Jill and Krista find the results convincing. They believe that the study correctly estimated how reducing elementary class size affected achievement scores in the context of Tennessee in the 1980s.

Most studies aren't simply relevant or irrelevant, or convincing or unconvincing. Rather, they must be judged on how relevant and convincing they are for addressing the problem at hand, relative to whatever alternative sources of information are available. When you have many studies on a topic, you can be picky, choosing ones that are more relevant and more convincing. But when there are few studies, you can often still learn something useful if you keep appropriate limitations in mind. The weight you place on a study's relevance and persuasiveness will vary with circumstances. Sometimes you are hoping to spark a creative brainstorming process or get general background, which means you don't have to be so picky. Other times, you may be making a high-stakes decision and care deeply about predicting whether a strategy will work in your situation. In that case, you need to be certain that the strategy caused the outcome in the study. Definitions of what constitutes good research (see chapter 4), like ESSA's tiers of evidence, are geared toward those one-time, high-stakes decisions—but those decisions account for just a fraction of the time education leaders interact with research.

> Task force leader Erin Frazier is excited by the idea of the greetings strategy described in "Attendance Playbook" and used at Hillside last year. She is thinking about pitching it to all the elementary schools in the district. But before she tries to get people on board, she wants to learn more about the evidence behind the strategy. She makes a note to see what the team can learn from Hillside's own data and reads the playbook's summary of the academic research:
>
> > A 2018 study of middle school students by University of Minnesota researchers found that when teachers used this technique at the classroom door, academic engagement increased by 20 percentage points and disruptive behavior decreased by 9 percentage points, when compared to classrooms without the greetings. Researchers estimate this adds the equivalent of another hour of engagement to the school day. In the 2018 study, teachers greeted the students by name at the door or with a handshake or nod of the head. They also reminded students to start their work or reflected on some issue a student might be having. With younger children, some teachers ask if the student wants a handshake, a high five or a hug. Others develop unique, often elaborate greetings for each child.[1]
>
> When she first skimmed the description in "Attendance Playbook," she thought the finding was about the effects of greeting students at the door. As she returns and reads more closely, she sees that teachers were also reminding students to stay on task or reflecting on "some issue a student might be having." Erin wonders how much time these additional tasks took. Was any training required? Would teachers be on board? She notices that the summary doesn't mention attendance—just academic engagement and disruptive behavior. And are those 20 and 9 percentage point changes large or small? Should they expect similar impacts in their own district if they tried the strategy?
>
> Erin has enough questions that she decides it's time to go to the original source. Luckily, the report provides a full citation for the article being reviewed, "Positive Greetings at the Door: Evaluation of a Low-Cost, High-Yield Proactive Classroom Management Strategy," but the link has a paywall.[2] She then enters the title of the article on Google Scholar and finds five versions, two of which provide links to free pdfs. Success! She won't need to ask her nephew who is in college to download it for her; nor will she have to write an awkward email to the authors asking for the paper. (Erin doesn't know that authors love to share their work. Feel free to email authors and not bother your nephew.)

JUDGING RELEVANCE

It can be tempting to dismiss evidence because "our district is different," but we encourage you to push yourself to ask why and how much any differences might matter. To determine how relevant a piece of research is for your situation, start by figuring out what the study is actually investigating, and for whom. You'll want to ask detailed questions about the strategy, the outcomes, any other key measures observed in the data, the sample, and the setting (see the sidebar "What Makes Research Relevant?").

What Makes Research Relevant?

STRATEGY

Information to extract from the study: What specific strategy is studied, and what is the alternative? For example, if it's a tutoring strategy, who is the tutor? What is the tutor-to-student ratio? How frequent and how long are the sessions?

Where to find it in the study: The strategy will be defined in general terms throughout the paper. Details may be in separate sections, appendices, or footnotes, with key terms like *treatment* (following medical terminology), *intervention*, or *implementation*.

Follow-up questions to ask yourself: What resources are required? What is the strategy being compared to—practice as usual or something else? Is the strategy studied similar to the strategy of interest to me? How or why would any differences matter for implementation? For impact on outcomes?

OUTCOMES

Information to extract from the study: What specific outcomes are studied? For example, does the study describe not just which test the scores are from, but also how it measured them?" Are the scores proficiency rates or average scaled scores? Were the scores for all students or only those who were academically behind? In what subjects and grade levels were the tests given? Were the tests state assessments or formative ones?

Where to find it in the study: The data section will describe all outcomes studied; the abstract and the results section will highlight some of them. Important outcomes that are not included in the study are often listed under a limitations section or in a paragraph outlining needs "for further research."

Follow-up questions to ask yourself: Were the tests state assessments, district-selected formative assessments, or something else? Why?

OTHER VARIABLES

Information to extract from the study: What other variables are included? For example, does the study include demographic information or prior test scores for students? What about data about the school, the district, or the state?

Where to find it in the study: The sample or data sections will usually describe all the main variables included in the study. A limitations section or a section titled "For Further Research" will highlight what's missing and how it matters for interpreting the research.

Follow-up questions to ask yourself: Does the study include control variables for factors that are likely to influence both participation in the strategy and the outcome I'm interested in? Does it recognize that different strategies might work better for different students?

SAMPLE

Information to extract from the study: What is the sample? How is it formed? (Which students, classes, schools?) Is anyone systematically excluded? How large is the sample? What is the composition of the sample in terms of academic performance, socioeconomic status, students with disabilities, English language learners, race, ethnicity, gender, and any other groups of interest? What is the composition of the sample in terms of teachers' experience levels and training?

Where to find it in the study: The sample or data sections will usually describe which *observations* (e.g., students, classes, or schools) are in the study. Check for appendices and footnotes, and for tables labeled "Descriptive statistics" or "Sample characteristics." A limitations section or a section titled "For Further Research" may highlight how the composition of the sample matters for interpreting the research.

Follow-up questions to ask yourself: How similar is the sample to the population of interest to me? If it is different, will I be able to implement the strategy well? Is a well-implemented strategy likely to affect outcomes in my population in the same way that it did in the sample population studied?

SETTING

Information to extract from the study: What is the setting? Has the study provided information on locality (rural, suburban, or urban); the size of the district (e.g., number of schools); the type of school (e.g., traditional, vocational, charter, alternative); union contracts or other labor relationships; governance structure (e.g., how charter schools are authorized); state policy; when the research was conducted; which academic standards were in place; educational philosophy (e.g., Montessori, No Excuses charter schools)?

Where to find it in the study: The sample or data sections will usually describe the setting.

Follow-up questions to ask yourself: How close is the setting to mine? If it is different, in what ways might that matter?

The first three topics—the strategy, the outcome, and other variables—all relate to how the concept you want to learn about is recorded, quantified, and analyzed in the study. A concept, as measured in data, is called a *variable*; that's because its values *vary* across different records in the data set.

> Dwayne Taylor wants to know if teachers are staying away from rural districts because they feel socially isolated, but he has no data measuring exactly this concept. He does, however, have access to data on which high schools were attended by recent education graduates in the state university system. He can compare the locations of those schools with where the graduates are currently teaching to create a new variable indicating whether a teacher is teaching in the county in which he or she attended high school. This new variable could be helpful for investigating Dwayne's hypothesis, if he is willing to assume that people who teach near where they went to high school feel less isolated.

Notice how what you actually observe—for example, not whether teachers feel socially isolated, but whether they are working near where they graduated from high school—differs from what you care about, and consider how meaningful the difference is likely to be. Thinking carefully about how closely your data (as measured with your variable) relate to what you ideally want to measure is important, whether you are thinking about strategies (e.g., class-size reduction in general versus going from twenty-two to fifteen students); outcomes (e.g., school climate versus a score on one survey with a low response rate); or other factors (e.g., poverty versus free or reduced-price lunch eligibility).

The Strategy (and the Alternative)

Any study of how a strategy affects outcomes is ultimately a study of how one strategy affects outcomes *relative to something else*. You have to find out what the strategy is, and what the "something else" is, to know exactly what correlates with any differences you see in outcomes. You also need to know what is required to implement the strategy—the necessary resources, including people, time, and money—to decide if the strategy is feasible in your situation. If the strategy is not practicable, then all the evidence on impact is irrelevant for you. The implementation questions from chapter 1 are a good place to begin for thinking through the question of feasibility.

From the start, Erin knew she needed a relatively quick and easy intervention for chronic absenteeism her school district. The high-five greeting practice from the Edutopia video seems to fit the bill. But she needs to know exactly what's involved with this practice to determine just how quick and easy it really is. As she reads about the greetings strategy, she realizes it involves more than just welcoming students each day.

Erin scans the "Positive Greetings at the Door" article she successfully found online for free, stopping for a closer read at the section headed "Intervention." It turns out that the strategy involved two other components: "providing both individual student and whole class pre-corrective statements to facilitate students' successful transition into the classroom setting" and "a positive reinforcement contingency . . . so teachers contingently recognize students' behavior for being on time to class."[3] Erin thinks that the first component would, if done well, probably require a big shift for teachers who had been struggling with classroom management. But seeing that the participating teachers were prepared for the program with just two one-hour training sessions is heartening: she could probably develop something similar in-house. She is glad she went beyond the headlines to see the other components of the strategy.

Teachers were selected for the study if they had low student engagement in their classes. Of these selected teachers, some were randomly chosen to participate in the strategy, while others (the control group) were not. The control group started off by meeting with administrators to discuss classroom-management issues for two hours, the same amount of time that the Positive Greetings at the Door teachers spent training on the strategy at the start of the study. Both groups also had two follow-up sessions. From Erin's perspective, the study just became much more convincing. It didn't compare Positive Greetings at the Door strategy with no strategy or even with "practice as usual." It compared Positive Greetings at the Door with exactly the type of relatively unstructured alternative she had been considering.

As Erin attempts to figure out how much the strategy would cost, she realizes she needs to learn a lot more about how it would be implemented. Would the schools want to involve all teachers in the strategy, as is done at Hillside, or just those with lower levels of academic engagement in their classrooms, as was done in the Positive Greetings at the Door study? Who would conduct the trainings and follow-up sessions, and how much time would it take? The schools in the study had a teacher on special assignment already working with other teachers on equity issues, but who would do this in Lincoln's schools? If staff already employed by the district, rather than a contractor, did the trainings, there would be no invoice to pay—but there would still be the opportunity cost of whatever activity the coaching displaced. Estimating the cost of a strategy, aside from helping you budget, is a great way to get ahead of potential implementation challenges.

The Outcomes

People often talk about an intervention as good or bad, effective or ineffective—but the question is, good or bad at what? Usually, their opinion involves whether the intervention improved some sort of student outcome, but not necessarily the one you care about. For example, an evaluation of the Success for All program found positive effects on alphabetics, a relatively low-level reading skill, but its impact on reading comprehension and achievement was less conclusive.[4] Whether or not you care about a particular outcome, like word attack, depends on your local needs and values. Either way, you deserve to know precisely which positive outcome is supported by evidence. This is important for harder-to-measure things too, such as reducing inequality, improving school climate, or increasing parent engagement. All these concepts can be measured well, or not so well. You need to understand exactly how a concept is measured in the evidence you're interpreting to know how closely it corresponds to your own goals.

> Erin learns that the study of classroom greetings in "Attendance Playbook" doesn't examine attendance or chronic absenteeism: "Academic engagement increased by 20 percentage points and disruptive behavior decreased by 9 percentage points . . . So far, none of the research into classroom greetings makes a direct link to school absenteeism, but there is ample research connecting better attendance to student engagement and connections to caring adults."[5] This conclusion makes sense to Erin, but she nevertheless makes a note to check out the research on attendance and engagement later.

This lack of research on attendance is disappointing to Erin, but at least she knows that the researchers didn't intentionally exclude a negative finding. She also sees that the academic engagement and disruptive behavior measures came from in-class coding of student time. From the descriptive statistics section, she learns that before the intervention, the students were observed spending 59 percent of their time academically engaged; after their teachers implemented the strategy, students spent 80 percent of their time academically engaged. In contrast, in the comparable classrooms that didn't implement the greetings, student engagement changed little over that time frame, from 55 percent to 60 percent of the time observed. As the authors note, the increase for the classrooms that implemented the strategy "corresponds to . . . an additional hour of engagement over the course of a 5-hr instructional day."[6]

Other Measures

Researchers rely on variables other than strategies and outcomes to select their samples and to "control for" things (that is, make comparisons among similar observations, as we'll discuss more shortly). They also may use other variables to see if some strategies are more effective for some types of students (or teachers or schools) than others or to describe the context of a study and help readers judge its relevance.

Just like measures of strategies and outcomes, these other variables need to be good measures of what you care about. This means there's no right set of other variables you should expect to see in every study. But two variables are so common and useful that we want to mention them here: prior achievement and free or reduced-price lunch (FRPL) eligibility. In studies using administrative student-level data, these two measures are often used as proxies for the vast amount of student information that we *can't* observe. They are imperfect substitutes, to be sure, but they still add a lot of information. Studies analyzing the effects of a strategy on student outcomes aim to compare two things: student outcomes *with* the strategy and some best guess of what the outcomes would have been *without* it. Using information about students' past outcomes is a great way to make that guess more precise.

Most often, the outcome we're interested in is student achievement, or test scores. Researchers often include prior test scores as a control variable in analyses of the impact of a strategy on current test scores. This way, the analysis accounts for the impact that students' prior ability level and educational opportunities might have on their current outcomes, independent of the strategy. (Later in this chapter, we'll describe how to control for a variable, and in chapter 5, we'll discuss how to analyze test scores.)

By contrast, FRPL eligibility measures whether a student participates in the US Department of Agriculture's school lunch program. FRPL eligibility has appeared in student-level administrative data sets for decades, as well as in school- and district-level data published by the National Center for Education Statistics. Because schools do not have other student-level data on family income, this variable is a standby for researchers. And, researchers aside, FRPL eligibility is an important variable for districts because of financing formulas that the states use for schools and because of the states' reporting requirements. To make the most of FRPL data, research suggests constructing multiyear measures of eligibility; for example, consider how many years a third grader has been eligible since kindergarten, rather than simply whether the student is eligible in third grade. These measures identify the highest-risk students better than do the measures of disadvantage at one point in time.[7]

The introduction and rapid expansion of the US Department of Agriculture's Community Eligibility Provision has changed how students in many high-poverty schools qualify for free meals—essentially eliminating the paperwork for parents and deeming all students eligible for free meals if their schools participate in the Community Eligibility Provision option. Schools' increased participation in this option makes the use of FRPL data to measure economic disadvantage harder, because now the data mean different things, depending on where the school is located.[8] Whether you are looking to FRPL status for research or policy reasons, be sure you understand what it measures in its specific context. Its meaning varies from state to state and is changing in real time as states adjust to the new requirements.

The Sample

> Erin turns to the question of who was studied in the research on Positive Greetings at the Door. The sample included ten teachers and 203 students. One thing catches her eye: the strategy was implemented in a randomly selected subset of classrooms the principal had suggested because of their high level of "disruptive and off-task behaviors."[9] As Erin thinks about what the study would mean for the Lincoln School District, she wonders if Positive Greetings at the Door was so effective because it taught a few solid classroom-management practices to teachers who were starting out at a disadvantage. The study noted that only one of the teachers in the sample had taken a classroom-management class as part of her training. Erin doubts such a small dose of classroom-management training would improve engagement as much for teachers who already have those basics down. When she makes her way to the discussion section, she sees that the authors have flagged this very issue.

Two issues jump out with the sample in the Positive Greetings at the Door paper: its composition (as Erin noted, including only teachers whose students were less engaged to start), and its size, with ten classrooms. Is ten classrooms a lot or a little? There's no hard-and-fast rule here, and it depends in part on what other research is available. If few other studies have been conducted on the topic, a study of ten classrooms is better than no information. But where many studies exist, you might want to look for ones with larger or more representative samples. The Hillside Elementary team that was inspired by the Edutopia video had read a short Edutopia article about it. The article began with a discussion of sample size: "A widely cited 2007 study claimed that teachers greeting students at the classroom door led to a 27 percentage point increase in academic engagement. The problem? It included just three students. Now a new, much larger and more credible study—comprising 203 students in 10 classrooms—validates that claim: Greeting students at the door sets a positive tone and can increase engagement and reduce disruptive behavior."[10]

Unlike the Edutopia writer, the authors of the Positive Greetings at the Door study considered the sample size small and a limitation of their work. They noted that the small sample "lessens generalizability of the study findings," and they urged future research to replicate the strategy with a larger and more diverse sample.

The Setting

Erin thinks that the demographics of the middle schools in the Positive Greetings at the Door study look pretty similar to those in the Lincoln School District. And she isn't so worried about an exact demographic match, because the basic idea—that building relationships between students and teachers promotes engagement—doesn't seem to depend on student demographics. She has been considering the strategy just for elementary schools, but now she thinks her middle school teachers might also be interested in this evidence. She wonders if the district might try the strategy in the high school as well, but she thinks it will be too hard to get those teachers on board when none of the evidence came from a high school. They might be more convinced if things go well at the middle school this year.

When you are judging a study's relevance, try to isolate what would be different in your setting. Then consider how those differences would—or wouldn't—affect both your ability to implement the strategy and the outcomes of a well-implemented strategy. Here are some examples:

- A study of classroom practices that support phonemic awareness can inform practice in a rural district, even if it was conducted in an urban district. Meanwhile, a study of providing students with books over the summer is less likely to be relevant in an environment where students have plentiful access to books at home already—even if both settings are urban.

- A study was conducted in a huge district to see how giving more discretion to school as opposed to district leaders changed practice.

- A study of the effects of the length of the school day is not helpful right now if your collective bargaining agreement prohibits changing the length of the day. But it could be helpful in negotiating the next agreement.

- A study of how a program of intensive support for struggling readers was conducted in all grades of a K–5 school with a highly skilled reading specialist and additional staff dedicated to the program. The study is unlikely to be useful in predicting how the program would work in a school lacking the capacity to implement it with as many resources as the study school used.

If you have a surplus of studies, focus on those closer to your own circumstances, with larger samples, where the strategy and outcomes better match your ideas. This advice relies on researchers doing their jobs by clearly describing all these factors. Ideally, as statistician Elizabeth Stuart and colleagues suggest, researchers would be explicit about which aspects of context matter for a strategy's success.[11] But if you have only a few choices, some information and a healthy dose of common sense is better than no information. Over time, you can build your own supply of highly relevant research by evaluating your work using your own data. With this in mind, Erin decides to find out if the district can use its own data to learn anything about Hillside's experience with the greetings strategy.

JUDGING CONVINCINGNESS

The history of education research is notorious for failing to use study designs that can produce convincing findings.[12] This section explains how to decide if evidence is convincing. We explain a few technical terms that you will run across in evidence requirements, but unless we say otherwise, think of the words we use as having their typical English meanings rather than technical definitions.

While most evidence aggregators, such as the What Works Clearinghouse (WWC), are much better at assessing a study's convincingness than they are at assessing its relevance, their internal standards are necessarily somewhat arbitrary. You might prefer a study that is moderately relevant and moderately convincing over one that's irrelevant, even if it's quite convincing. But the WWC might exclude your preferred study because it isn't convincing enough by the clearinghouse's measure. This section gives you the tools to quickly estimate how convincing something is for yourself, so you can draw on a broader range of research.

These criteria apply to large-scale quantitative research that tests hypotheses. While studies won't always describe their approaches with the term *hypothesis test*, how they describe their research design and results will tip you off. The research design could include keywords such as t-*tests, differences in means, regression analysis, t-test, experiment*, and *randomized controlled trial.* And if the results mention statistical terms including *statistical significance,* p-*values, effect size*, or *confidence interval*, the study tests hypotheses.

For other types of research such as descriptive or qualitative work, you'll find some studies that are more convincing and others that are less convincing—but you would judge them using different criteria.

We focus on two main and totally separate ideas for judging research. The first is the extent to which you believe one thing caused another and is not simply related to it. The second is assessing the likelihood that a finding is due to chance, statistically speaking.

The Distinction Between Correlation and Causation

If you see a large crowd on the subway platform, the next train will probably come soon: crowd size and wait time are correlated. But if you bring a large crowd onto the platform, the train won't come any sooner. This is just one example of how correlation doesn't always reflect causation. For a study to convince you that a strategy *causes* a change in an outcome, you need to see a compelling comparison. Look for two features:

- The study needs some groups (students, classrooms, teachers, schools, etc.) that participated in the strategy and some that did not. This requirement could include the comparison of at least two groups (with or without some defined strategy) or different observations experiencing or receiving different amounts of something, like class size or spending per pupil.

- The study must also have a way to account for the fact that people who choose to participate in a strategy are probably different from those who don't. We turn to this next.

Challenges of Showing Cause and Effect

Imagine your district's gifted program begins in fourth grade and you want to know how or if participation in the program affects achievement. If you saw that students in the program scored higher on the fourth-grade state tests than other students did, you wouldn't conclude that the gifted program *caused* the scores to be higher. That's because you know that the types of students selected for the gifted program in the first place are likely to score well on the state test—even if they don't enroll in the program. More generally, people who volunteer or are specially selected to participate in a program or strategy are different from those who don't. We're trying to see how the strategy (e.g., the gifted program) itself contributes to outcomes (e.g., fourth-grade test scores). Unfortunately, those differences behind who participates may be at least partly responsible for any differences in outcomes across the groups. This general problem is called *selection bias*.

A quick note on what we do and don't mean by bias in the term *selection bias*: there's plenty of bias in who participates in different programs, often along the lines of accountability subgroups related to race, ethnicity, class, disability, and English language fluency. These types of bias are major problems for equity. The kind of bias we mean in the statistical term *selection bias*, though, is about getting a systematically incorrect ("biased") answer to how large an impact a strategy has, not about unfairness or inequity in who gets picked to participate. Selection bias isn't a problem for students; it's a problem for researchers, because this sort of bias makes it hard to tell when one thing causes another.

Any time a question asks how some strategy *affects* an outcome, it is your job as a reader to wonder why some students, teachers, schools, or systems participated in the strategy and why some comparison group did not. Could this reason affect the outcome directly, independently from the strategy? If so, is there some way you could account for it?

One of the team members reports to Erin: "There seems to be a lot of research showing that students who miss many days in kindergarten do worse in first grade." That's pretty compelling when we're thinking about how many resources we want to devote to these efforts. If we could get the attendance rate up for these kindergarteners, they would be on a more secure academic path."

Erin doubts this logic. "Whatever they have going on outside of school that led to them missing so much school in the first place probably also made them do poorly in first grade," she says, "not just the fact that they missed all that school during kindergarten." Erin

> is thinking that many issues could affect both chronic absenteeism and test scores—things like homelessness, a parent's mental illness, or a child's undiagnosed learning disability.

In the study of positive greetings at the door, the teachers in the sample were randomly assigned to either training on the strategy or a general classroom-management chat with a school administrator. But what if a study instead compared academic engagement in classrooms for two groups: a group where teachers had signed up for the training and a group where teachers had opted out? Teachers who signed up might be more interested in their professional development than other teachers were, and this attitude might also improve engagement. Or they might be struggling, and their academic engagement rates could reflect their other troubles. Either way, it's not an apples-to-apples comparison. Because it's often hard to measure reasons driving participation, selection bias presents a vexing problem for research. Luckily, a range of statistical approaches helps reduce the problem of selection bias. We turn to these next.

Randomization as the Gold Standard

Medical science has long recognized randomization as an unsurpassed means of proving cause and effect. In 2019, economists Abhijit Banerjee, Esther Duflo, and Michael Kremer won the Nobel Prize in Economics for their work using randomized controlled trials (RCTs) to study topics in development economics, including education.[13] RCTs use randomization—think of a figurative coin toss, or a literal random number generator or other lottery mechanism—to assign participants to either a treatment group that participates in some strategy or a control group experiencing some alternative. When participants are randomly assigned their participation status, rather than choosing it for themselves, the possibility of selection bias is eliminated.

We offer a few caveats on RCTs. First, watch the language. All RCTs are experiments, but not all experiments are RCTs; similarly, all RCTs randomly assign participants to a treatment or control status, but not all groups referred to as treatment and control groups are constructed randomly. Next, consider relevance. Because randomization is carried out only among subjects who are willing to be randomized, good analyses of RCTs explain their sample and setting so that readers can decide how relevant the finding is for them. The Positive Greetings at the Door study convincingly demonstrated the effect of the intervention for teachers whose students showed low academic engagement to start, but we haven't learned anything about what to expect from the strategy in other types of classrooms. The study also took place in a district that was willing and able to participate, so we don't know how the approach would work in districts without such capacity.

Showing Cause and Effect Without Randomization

Despite the statistical benefits of randomization, it can pose logistical, political, and ethical challenges, so you won't often find an RCT speaking to your question. And sometimes you'll prefer a more relevant study, even if it means sacrificing the strong causal interpretation that an RCT allows. Most of the time, you'll find studies using other research methods, and you'll want to see if they can persuade you that they have sufficiently countered the role of selection bias. To do this, they should explain intuitively (in words, not just equations) why one group was in some way *arbitrarily* (so not quite as good as randomly) more likely to be exposed to a strategy than some other group. Focus on the intuition over the jargon—when researchers happen upon a situation that lends itself to good comparisons, they sell it to their readers. And if they don't mention some source of arbitrary (sometimes called *quasi-experimental*) variation, you'll want to think hard about the selection bias you would expect in that scenario.

Why might one group be arbitrarily more likely to participate in a strategy than another group would? Look for formal changes in policy or practice that include a specific date for the change, rules that involve cutoffs for assigning resources or students, or differential treatment of similar places for arcane reasons. Consider some plausible situations:

■ A state mandates that districts offer full-day prekindergarten for all students beginning in 2015. Not all students who started kindergarten in 2015 or earlier had access to full-day prekindergarten; all students who started kindergarten in 2016 or later did.

■ A district has guidelines for maximum class of 27 students in first grade. One school has 108 first graders and creates four classes with 27 students each. Another school, this one with 110 first graders, has to create five classes with 22 students each.[14] The difference in class sizes across schools is essentially randomly created by the combination of district policy and grade-level enrollment at each school from year to year, not parent choices, local resources, or other factors.

Such arbitrary ways of assigning access to resources are often referred to as quasi-experiments, and researchers use a range of statistical methods to take advantage of them. (Chapters 5 and 7 give examples of how they might apply in your classroom, school, or district). But a so-called quasi-experimental method is only as good as the circumstances it exploits, so focus on the quality of the comparison rather than being impressed by the methods. As a bonus, you can skip all the dense statistics related to discussion of the difference in differences, interrupted time series, propensity scores, matching methods, instrumental variables, synthetic controls, regression discontinuity designs, and so on.

While researchers rejoice when they encounter arbitrary circumstances, many important questions don't lend themselves to this approach. The rest of the time, the best approach is to control for the differences (those that you can measure with your data) that you suspect may influence both who chooses to participate in a strategy and (independently) the outcome of interest. Controlling for something just means seeing how other things vary while you hold one thing constant. For example, imagine you want to compare taking the bus to school and walking in relation to chronic absenteeism, but you know that economically disadvantaged students in your district are more likely to live on a bus route and that research has shown a link between poverty and chronic absenteeism. That is, you want to look at the relationship between bus riding and absenteeism, but you want to take out of the mix the correlation between poverty and bus riding. To do this, you could examine the relationship between bus riding and chronic absenteeism first for students who are FRPL eligible and then examine it separately for students who are not FRPL eligible. In multiple-regression analysis, you can control for many variables at once.

How many control variables a study includes is not important. What matters is the extent to which those controls help form convincing comparisons—which you must determine using common sense and your professional expertise. Even when a study convincingly controls for some concerning differences between those who participate in an intervention and those who don't, ask yourself if other differences probably remain.

Assessing a Study for Cause and Effect

It would be delightful if authors consistently described how well their studies determine cause and effect. But researchers will often go back and forth in tone in a single study, at times using language careful to avoid implications of causation, then slipping in a few keywords that directly suggest cause and effect. If the researcher seems to be taking pains to avoid causal implications in one place, that's the language to heed. (See "Words to watch out for on claims of cause and effect.") And even when researchers are fastidious about their language, translators of research (including the editors who write headlines) often unintentionally paraphrase careful original language about correlations in ways that introduce substantive differences in meaning.

Consider how "Attendance Playbook" described one study of school climate and attendance.[15] It said the study found "a direct correlation between alienating school climates and student absenteeism," and noted which aspects of school climate were "most closely linked to attendance."[16] These words don't imply cause and effect. Researchers and translators are much more likely to err in the direction of overstating causation—so when you see correlational terms like those just quoted in "Attendance Playbook," there's no need to check further.

Words to Watch Out for on Claims of Cause and Effect	
NO CLAIMS OF CAUSE AND EFFECT	**CLAIMS OF CAUSE AND EFFECT**
Researchers who want to be careful and transparent use this type of language to warn readers away from reading too much causation into their findings. • We observe an *association* between achievement and attendance. • Achievement and attendance are positively *correlated*. • There is a positive *relationship* (or, even, a strong positive relationship) between achievement and attendance. • Achievement is *linked to* attendance. Also look for general disclaimers like these: • We cannot fully account for *selection bias* in our results. • We rely on *observational* data. • We rely on *cross-sectional* data.	The types of statements in the left column can morph into stronger claims of causation like these in the right column—though their claims may not be supported by the analysis. • When attendance increases, achievement *follows* (or *improves*). • Improvements in attendance *lead to* (or *result in*) increased achievement. • Better attendance *causes* (or *yields*) improvements in achievement. • Test score increases *resulted* from (or are a *consequence* of) improved attendance.

But what about when you are seriously considering a strategy and need to predict how it would work for you? Even if the study uses causal language, check the analysis yourself. You need to be convinced that participation in the strategy is what led to any differences between those who participated and those who didn't—not just being the type of student, teacher, or school that was likely to participate. Because few studies provide slam-dunk proof of cause and effect, it makes little sense to limit yourself to those that do—especially when many other studies do a pretty good, albeit not definitive, job. But when a study does not directly address your concerns about selection bias head on, be wary.

Effect Sizes

Effect sizes don't mean that research proves cause and effect. We mention them in this section only because of their confusing name. The effect size is a measure of the strength of an association between participation in a strategy and an outcome that comes from comparing outcomes between participants and nonparticipants; the term *association size* would be more accurate. The benefit of effect size is that it is a standardized metric that allows the reader to compare the magnitude of the associations from strategies measured in different units (for example, how class-size reductions versus tutoring interventions are associated with test scores).[17] But the term *effect* is confusing, because you can calculate an effect size for any association or correlation, even if you are sure that the association does *not* represent cause and effect.

Many readers are familiar with effect size through the writing of John Hattie, professor at University of Melbourne, Australia. In his book *Visible Learning*, Hattie notes the important distinction between correlation and causation—but his ranking of "influences and effect sizes" on student outcomes has sowed confusion.[18] There is a widespread and false impression that an intervention with a higher effect size is somehow better than one with a lower one or that an intervention should have an effect size greater than 0.4 (the average effect size in Hattie's sample).[19]

Why is this impression incorrect? To start, Hattie did not distinguish studies whose designs allow for claims of cause and effect from those that simply measured correlations. It would be quite challenging for Hattie to give any such indication, because he was doing a meta-analysis of existing meta-analyses; he was essentially taking all the sausage in the supermarket and turning it into a giant new sausage. If one single study convincingly shows cause and effect with an effect size of 0.3, that is more useful than an unconvincing study with an effect size of 0.5. And there is nothing magical about 0.4. That's just the average effect size in the studies and meta-analyses Hattie analyzed. As Matthew Kraft, professor of education at Brown University, advises, look for convincing evidence of cause and effect, feasibility, and cost-effectiveness relative to the next-best alternative strategies, not the biggest effect size or an effect size greater than 0.4.[20] For more on this statistical issue, see the sidebar "Interpreting Effect Sizes" in chapter 6.

The Deceptive Authority of Statistical Significance

Many studies tout the statistical significance of their results. But we haven't even mentioned statistical significance yet, because it has nothing to do with cause and effect.

Statistical significance is all about figuring out whether a difference you see in your sample is real or not—that is, if the difference in your sample is probably not simply due to chance. No, this isn't the technical definition, but it's all you need. If you want technical details (trust us, it's hard to say more than that one sentence without getting into them), check out Khan Academy or any statistics textbook (also see "Statistics and Research Methods" in the Further Readings section at the end of this book).

Researchers don't want to say that a difference is real when it isn't, so they set a high bar for making this kind of claim. That's where statistical significance and *p*-values come in. When you conduct a statistical analysis, the software spits out a number called a *p*-value along with whatever difference (between groups) or effect (of some strategy) you are estimating. As education writers Denise-Marie Ordway and Holly Yettick explain, "Big values of *p* are evidence supporting the idea that the results were due to chance. Small values of p are evidence against the idea that chance explains the outcome."[21] An important note: if the sample is small or the value of a key variable doesn't fluctuate much, it's hard to detect statistically significant differences. If a *p*-value is less than or equal to 0.05, researchers will usually say that the difference is statistically significant; if it's larger, they'll say it's insignificant.

If this cutoff value seems arbitrary to you, you're in good company. A number of scientific associations are moving away from reliance on statistical significance as a binary concept.[22] One alternative, a *confidence interval,* describes the range of plausible impacts based on what we know from the sample studied. A statistically insignificant difference or association is simply one that is indistinguishable from zero—meaning zero falls within the confidence interval. Still, statistical *insignificance* can mean two very different things. Statistically insignificant results can be quite useful when they reveal strong *evidence of no effect* or association, by showing even small potential effects or associations are extremely unlikely (for example, language like "we can rule out any effect size greater than 0.01 or less than –0.02"). Statistically insignificant differences are less useful when they deliver *no evidence of effect* or association, without being able to rule out the potential of larger associations (for example, "we can rule out only those effect sizes greater than 0.9 or less than –0.7"). If a confidence interval includes zero, as both of our examples do, by definition the impact of the program is statistically insignificant. But there's a world of difference between the first example, where the range of possible impacts is small (and therefore we are quite certain the impact is zero), and the second, where it is large (and therefore we're not sure whether the impact is zero, well above zero, or well below). Dismissing all statistically insignificant findings as uninformative means throwing out the valuable distinction between wide and narrow confidence intervals that include zero.

BEYOND RELEVANT AND CONVINCING: PRACTICAL SIGNIFICANCE

Keisha Marks, the data manager for Lincoln Public Schools, reports back to Erin on how chronic absenteeism varies by bus access: the average absenteeism rate is 13.6 percent for walkers and 10.6 percent for students on a bus route. Erin asks Keisha if this difference is meaningful. Erin didn't expect them to be the same, but she's not sure how different would be different enough to consider a policy like expanding the bus routes to serve more students. There's a lot to consider: the cost, the schedules for other schools, the length of the bus ride for all the students. But Erin doesn't even want to start thinking through all these details if the calculated differences aren't real, and she believes there's a way to use statistics to check.

Keisha responds, "Sure, there's a *t*-test. I can run it for you right now in Excel." (You can also find *t*-test calculators online.) "But it's going to tell you if the difference is likely due to chance in the sampling, not if it's big. And it's also not going to tell you if the bus access is responsible for the difference you see."

"Whoa, slow down," says Erin. "Can we do one thing at a time there?"

Keisha smiles. "Sure. I'll start with the chance part. There's the difference you see in the table: 13.6 minus 10.6 is 3.0 percentage points. The *t*-test can tell you if you'd be likely to see that big a difference in your data if there truly is no relationship between riding the bus and chronic absenteeism."

"Okay, and the other part?" Erin asks. "One group takes the bus and the other doesn't. Isn't it pretty straightforward that the bus access is causing the difference?"

Keisha sighs. "Unfortunately, the test only says *if* two things are different, not *why* they're different. There might be a reason that students who walk are more likely to be chronically absent—a reason that has nothing to do with walking but might be about the families or neighborhoods or something else—so putting them on a bus wouldn't change whatever made them absent in the first place."

Erin pulls up the map of school attendance boundaries. "It actually looks like that would be an issue. A lot of the walkers at Hillside travel a very short distance, from a low-income apartment complex. They could have a lot of home challenges that contribute to their absences but that have nothing to do with whether they take the bus."

"Right," Keisha says. "So, if we switch to a universal busing system, we really don't know what would happen with chronic absenteeism for walkers. I'm also guessing that even if it did decrease, that's a pretty small difference relative to the cost of additional busing."

See "What Makes Research Convincing?" for questions that will help you decide for yourself when Keisha's not around.

What Makes Research Convincing?

IT RELIES ON PURELY RANDOM DIFFERENCES TO *PROVE* CAUSATION . . .

Information to extract from the study: Does the study prove that the strategy *caused* the effect? This is strong language, so we apply the highest bar: did the study use a randomized controlled design?

Where to find it in the study: Authors are rightly proud of their use of a randomized controlled design, so key words noting that they have used this design often show up in the paper's abstract, if not the title itself.

Follow-up questions to ask yourself: Do I see the words *random, randomized, randomization,* or *lottery*? Do the authors show that the two groups were similar before the strategy was imposed (so that the lottery was indeed random)?

. . . OR IT MAKES STRONG COMPARISONS TO ACCOUNT FOR SELECTION BIAS.

Information to extract from the study: If the study doesn't use a randomized design, how well does the study account for selection bias? Without randomization, researchers find some way to compare outcomes with and without the strategy. Figure out what comparisons they make to decide how meaningful you find them.

Where to find it in the study: The best abstracts and introductions will give you some sense of how the study compares outcomes with and without the strategy, but you may need to go into the methods, analysis, or empirical strategy sections for more details. Fortunately, peer reviewers often require authors to explicitly acknowledge shortfalls. Authors often put these (relatively) juicy parts near the end of the paper, in the discussion, conclusion, or limitations sections.

Follow-up questions to ask yourself: Why do some groups participate in the strategy and not others? Might this difference affect outcomes independently? If the study compares outcomes for distinct groups, does the evidence (often in tables) show that the groups are comparable in other ways before the intervention?

FINDINGS ARE UNLIKELY TO BE DUE TO CHANCE

Information to extract from the study: Is the finding likely to be due to chance? This is totally separate from cause and effect. How likely would you be to get the same result if you drew a different sample from the overall population of data?

Where to find it in the study: Check the abstract, the introduction, or the results section. Scan for confidence intervals in the text, and look at the notes to tables to see how the *p*-values are derived.

Follow-up questions to ask yourself: If the result is statistically significant, ask, Does this likely reflect causation? How large is the effect? Is the intervention cost-effective? If not, ask, How likely is the result to be due to chance (what's the *p*-value?)? What magnitude of effect could I rule out (what's outside the confidence interval?)?

When research is relevant and convincing, it's time to move beyond the *direction* of the effect—for example, the Positive Greetings at the Door strategy had a positive impact on academic engagement—to its practical significance. This work requires thinking about *magnitudes*. For example, the study estimated that the Positive Greetings at the Door strategy increased academic engagement by about an hour per instructional day. You also need to tally the full set of costs described in chapter 1. Only then can you figure out the return on your investment in a strategy, rather than whether a strategy is evidence-based and works.

Ultimately, the practical significance of a study depends on how the strategy's costs and benefits compare with the next-best use of the money, be it the status quo or another option. Whether you are embarking on something new or are adjusting your current practice, you should consider evidence on more than one possible strategy so that you can shop around for the one that best meets your needs for cost and likely impact. It's just good common sense.

KEY TAKEAWAYS

* No magic cutoff determines whether a piece of research is relevant or convincing enough for your question. These qualities exist on a spectrum, and it's up to you to use common sense to make your own judgment. What is "close enough" to be informative depends on the stakes (how bad would it be to be wrong?) and the availability of other evidence (if two similar studies have conflicting findings, favor the one that is more relevant to your situation).

* Use the sidebar "What Makes Research Relevant?" to get a sense of how strong a match a large-scale quantitative study is a match for your needs, based on its sample, setting, and exact variables measured. You could think of this as a checklist of things to consider, but don't expect to check all the boxes.

* If you want maximal relevance, learn from your own data, as we'll cover in chapter 5. (And help others by sharing what you find!)

* Use the sidebar "What Makes Research Convincing?" to think about the predictive strength of a research finding. Better comparisons are what make some studies more convincing than others.

  • Knowing that a result is statistically significant tells you it is highly unlikely to be due to chance, but it doesn't tell you how meaningful it is.

  • Statistical significance is unrelated to cause and effect.

  • *Effect size* is a misnomer. It's just a standardized way to measure the size of correlations, but those correlations may or may not reflect cause and effect.

* Focus on practical significance, not statistical significance. Practical significance depends on research that is relevant and convincing and finds magnitudes of impact suggesting that a strategy is cost-effective and superior to other options.

APPLY YOUR LEARNING

☐ Return to your notes from chapter 1 to find your own question, in one sentence. Open the full text of the study you found in chapter 2.

☐ How was the sample in the study constructed? How large is it? Were observations included or excluded in any nonrandom way? How does the composition of the sample differ from the population you care about? How does this matter for how useful the study can be to you?

☐ What are the circumstances in the study you have chosen? Are they similar to yours? Why do you think the major differences between study's circumstances and your own will or will not matter? How much difference could the circumstances make in the outcome?

☐ Take a few minutes to figure out what the study's key variables, including the outcomes and the strategy, truly measure. How close is this conceptually to what will help answer your question?

☐ Do you think the study's findings are practically significant? Why or why not?

☐ Imagine, however unrealistically, an randomized controlled trial (RCT) that could help you answer your question. Would the RCT be hard to do? Why? What comparisons might help you investigate this causal claim without an RCT?

☐ If your question relates to a strategy versus a diagnosis, consider the implementation and cost questions you outlined in chapter 1. Does the study you have chosen have information about what resources will be required for implementation of the strategy? What information do you need to find elsewhere, and how can you get it? Consider calling the vendor, asking people who have implemented similar practices, contacting professional associations, or making your own guesstimates for each component.

4

UNDERSTAND WHAT ESSA
SAYS ABOUT EVIDENCE
(AND WHAT IT LEAVES OUT)

Now that you have a better sense of how to make sure the research you've un-covered is relevant and convincing, it's time to pause and consider the evidence mandates included in federal law. These mandates contrast somewhat with the common-sense approach to evidence put forward in this book. An examination of the provisions in ESSA will help you understand this contrast and will enable you to meet the federal mandates with relevant and convincing evidence, whether it's generated by you or by others.

We think our approach is common sense: use evidence whenever it can help, and ask questions to diagnose problems, assess the implementation of strategies, and evaluate their impact. And it's common sense to be sure that the research you rely on is both relevant and convincing. Unfortunately, this entire approach re-quires judgment—and judgment can't be legislated. So it's not surprising that evi-dence mandates take a different approach.

The Elementary and Secondary Education Act of 1965 governs federal grants for preK–12 education, including its largest funding stream, Title I. ESSA of 2015 is the most recent reauthorization of the law. Congress has long grappled with how to ensure that federal funds are spent well. ESSA's predecessor, the No Child Left Behind Act of 2001, encouraged the use of federal funds on projects supported by "scientifically based research," but only mandated it for Reading First funds. ESSA has dropped the "scientifically based research" language but now encourages (and, rarely, mandates) schools to spend funds in "evidence-based" ways. ESSA's standards for just what constitutes "evidence-based" vary by a school's circumstances.

As we will show, ESSA's view of evidence is narrow, technical, and rigid—the opposite of the common-sense framework described throughout the book. These differences, outlined in the sidebar "Common-Sense Evidence Versus ESSA Evidence," are utterly predictable. Give two people decades of training and hands-on research experience and tens of thousands of words, and you get common-sense evidence. Give Congress half a page to write a definition that auditors can enforce, and you get ESSA evidence.

Despite these drawbacks to ESSA's approach to evidence, education leaders should understand exactly what ESSA's evidence requirements mean. In this chapter, we show that you can apply our common-sense framework to obtaining relevant and convincing evidence while still complying with the ESSA requirements. And while the federal law doesn't restrict most of the decisions that leaders make, it has generated considerable confusion at the state and local levels. This chapter will help you understand how the status of your school affects evidence requirements under ESSA. We also explain the benefits of some types of research that ESSA doesn't discuss, and how drawing on a broader base of information might be helpful to you.

	Common-Sense Evidence Versus ESSA Evidence	
WHAT'S BEING COMPARED	**COMMON-SENSE EVIDENCE**	**ESSA REQUIREMENTS FOR STRONG, MODERATE, OR PROMISING EVIDENCE**
Definition of evidence	The body of information used to assess a claim	Any one study that meets specified technical requirements
Ways to use evidence	To diagnose problems, assess the implementation of strategies, and evaluate the impact of strategies on outcomes.	To evaluate the impact of strategies on outcomes
Criteria for judging evidence	By how relevant and convincing it is	By how convincing it is
Criteria for judging the likelihood that a result is due to chance	The body of other studies; replication of the result; confidence intervals or p-values; sample size	Statistical significance
Ways to judge whether a strategy *caused* an outcome	How effectively the study persuades you that the participants in the strategy, had they not partaken in the strategy, would have had outcomes similar to those of a comparison group that didn't participate	How its research methods map to ESSA's defined levels of evidence

HOW ESSA DEFINES *EVIDENCE-BASED*

This section describes, in plain language, the essential parts of ESSA's evidence definitions and requirements for schools. We are stripping down ESSA's language on evidence to what the law actually requires schools to do, ignoring mere recommendations about the use of evidence.[1] We're also skipping the (nonbinding) nonregulatory policy guidance, which offers a lot of optional nuance more consistent with our own views.[2] Finally, keep in mind that states and districts may add their own requirements about the use of evidence, for federal and other funds. Although these regulations are not covered explicitly here, the mapping of ESSA's requirements to the common-sense framework should help you interpret any additional rules you must adhere to in your locality and situation.

ESSA lays out four levels of evidence. According to the law's definition, an evidence-based activity demonstrates either (1) strong evidence, (2) moderate evidence, (3) promising evidence, or (4) "a rationale" based on encouraging findings and "ongoing [assessment] efforts" (see the sidebar "ESSA's Definition of Evidence" for more details). For schools receiving Section 1003 school improvement funds, ESSA applies a narrow definition of *evidence-based* (requiring any of the first three levels listed above). For all other schools, it applies a broader definition (allowing for any of the four levels of evidence-based activity). Strong, moderate, or promising evidence requires at least one existing study; in contrast, you can show "a rationale" for a strategy without any existing study. For most schools, the distinctions between these levels are irrelevant, because ESSA encourages but does not require the use of evidence-based strategies. And the law never requires strong or moderate evidence without permitting promising evidence as well.

The Letter of the Law

The following definition comes from the Every Student Succeeds Act (ESSA) of 2015, section 8101(21)(A). We added the italics for emphasis.

The term "evidence-based", when used with respect to a State, local educational agency, or school activity, means an activity, strategy, or intervention that—

(i) demonstrates a statistically significant effect on improving student outcomes or other relevant outcomes based on—

    (I) *strong evidence* from at least 1 well-designed and well-implemented experimental study;

(II) *moderate evidence* from at least 1 well-designed and well-implemented quasi-experimental study; or

(III) *promising evidence* from at least 1 well-designed and well-implemented correlational study with statistical controls for selection bias; or

(ii) (I) *demonstrates a rationale* based on high-quality research findings or positive evaluation that such activity, strategy, or intervention is likely to improve student outcomes or other relevant outcomes; and

(II) includes *ongoing efforts* to examine the effects of such activity, strategy, or intervention.

THE FIRST THREE LEVELS OF EVIDENCE: PROMISING, MODERATE, AND STRONG

According to Section 8101(21) of the law, under any of the top three levels of evidence (promising, moderate, and strong), any evidence-based "activity, strategy, or intervention" is required to show "a statistically significant effect on improving student outcomes or other relevant outcomes." Under ESSA, what determines whether something is counted as strong, moderate, or promising evidence is not just the nature of the effect but how the study is designed. Strong evidence relies on random assignment, moderate evidence requires a "quasi-experimental" approach, and promising evidence controls for confounders.

Statisticians could have a field day debating exactly what makes a study quasi-experimental and, consequently, whether a given study demonstrates moderate or promising evidence. What if you use a quasi-experimental method but without that desired quirky, naturally occurring arbitrariness determining who gets exposed to a strategy and who doesn't? Luckily, it doesn't matter in practice, at least under federal law. Even the most stringent definition of what makes a strategy evidence-based (that is, the definition applying to schools receiving Section 1003 funds) supports strategies at the strong, moderate, *or* promising level.

ESSA categorizes strategies by the research supporting them, and the law explicitly requires "at least 1 well-designed and well-implemented" study to match a strategy to a level of evidence; in other words, one study is sufficient under the law. Yet any given strategy is often the subject of multiple studies, often reaching different conclusions, so the law provides an incentive to cherry-pick studies. While it makes good sense to avoid a strategy with one piece of evidence supporting it and several other, more-credible studies refuting that finding, you are legally permitted to choose such a strategy. It's also easy to do this inadvertently: once you find a study that confirms your initial belief, it may feel like your work is done.

Mind the Gap: Ambiguity in ESSA

The law leaves a lot unsaid. For example:

- What's a study? Does it matter who wrote it and where—or if—it is published?
- What makes a study "well-designed" or "well-implemented"?
- What makes an effect statistically significant?

Congress didn't define these terms in the law—though the law includes plenty of other definitions, including for terms like *middle grades* and *professional development*. Nor do the terms have any secret official meaning among researchers other than what we've described in chapter 3. You have to use your judgment.

Here's our interpretation of these terms. A *study* is a research-based investigation of a topic. It doesn't matter whether or where it is published—Congress did not require a peer-reviewed study. Our earlier discussion about what makes research relevant and convincing is a useful way to define the ESSA terms *well-designed* and *well-implemented*, but no studies check all the boxes, so you need to exercise discretion. And as described in chapter 3, the most common level of confidence used to interpret statistical significance in education research is 95 percent (corresponding to a p-value of 0.05 or less), so we would generally use that as the standard for *statistical significance*.

Bridge the Gap

The US Department of Education's nonregulatory (and therefore nonbinding) policy guidance also attempts to fill some of these terminology gaps.[3] At points, this guidance is fairly nuanced and requires some research skills (which you now have) to interpret. Just as our guidelines for relevant and convincing evidence ask more of research than ESSA does, the federal guidance suggests that districts do much more than the law mandates. The policy, for example, recommends that "when available, strategies supported by higher levels of evidence should be prioritized."[4] As of 2020, no regulations (which would be legally binding) governed the definition of evidence in ESSA. You can check the department's website (www.ed.gov/ESSA) for the most recent guidance and regulations.

As recommended earlier, look for reviews of multiple studies to get the big picture, rather than relying on individual findings in isolation. (The US Department of Education's nonbinding policy guidance on ESSA's evidence provisions also suggests considering the body of research rather than just one study.)[5] In the process, you'll come across an individual study you can cite to support what you've concluded is the best strategy for you. In this way, you will also meet any evidence requirements that apply to you.

Let's say you've found something you think is a well-designed and well-implemented study. How do you know which level of evidence it falls under—so that you can determine whether it counts for your school? While evidence aggregators take on this task for some interventions, many strategies that are not branded educational products are overlooked in these sources. These unbranded strategies may still be perfectly legal under ESSA. The flowchart in figure 4.1 summarizes the material in this section (and the law) and walks you through the determination.

FIGURE 4.1

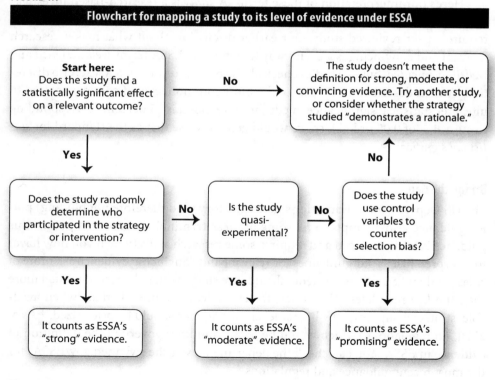

Flowchart for mapping a study to its level of evidence under ESSA

THE FOURTH LEVEL OF EVIDENCE: DEMONSTRATE A RATIONALE, AND GROW YOUR OWN

Unless you are dealing with Section 1003 (school improvement) funds, ESSA includes any strategy that "demonstrates a rationale" in its definition of evidence-based strategies. The law describes such a strategy as one that "demonstrates a rationale based on high-quality research findings or positive evaluation that such activity, strategy, or intervention is likely to improve student outcomes or other relevant outcomes and includes ongoing efforts to examine the effects of such activity, strategy, or intervention." The law does not define what makes "research findings" or "evaluations" different from "studies" or what constitutes "high quality"—but presumably this is a lower bar than the "promising" level of evidence. The clearest part of this definition is that it seeks to build the evidence base by requiring "ongoing efforts to examine the effects."

To use this option, first make the case for your strategy. You can do this with a combination of common sense, research that might not be ESSA-style (e.g., neuroscience, ethnography, or quantitative analysis that doesn't show cause and effect), and large-scale quantitative research that isn't sufficiently convincing and relevant to your situation to meet a higher level of evidence under ESSA. Once you've made the case, then plan to evaluate how the strategy works out—and follow through on the plan! Later in the book, you will learn about the tools for examining the effects of the strategy in your own circumstances.

ESSA's hinting that this approach is the lowest rank in the hierarchy of evidence seems misguided. In fact, Carrie has described ESSA's so-called fourth tier (or evidence level) as its "hidden gem."[6] Learning from your own data should be an integral part of your plan, whether or not existing research speaks to your question—not just a backup plan for when you can't find a study. There's simply no other way to know how your strategies work in your own environment.

In the longer run, this type of intentional planning and self-evaluation is how your work with students improves—and how the research base gets stronger. After all, the work you plan under the "lowest" level of evidence could become a study someone else turns to in the future for strong, moderate, or promising evidence. And you don't need to turn it into a long academic-style paper to share it. You could pitch a guest post to Edutopia, present at a regional meeting of your professional association or at researchED, or speak up on a conference call with other leaders in your state to share what you have found.

BEYOND THE OFFICIAL DEFINITIONS OF EVIDENCE

By focusing on statistical significance, ESSA is inherently defining evidence as large-scale quantitative studies that examine the effect of a particular educational strategy on student outcomes—studies of impact. But this implied definition excludes other, equally important types of research from a range of disciplines. This research can help you understand your problems, not just the impact of strategies. And it can help you make the case for whether a strategy "demonstrates a rationale," to qualify for the fourth level of evidence under ESSA.

Basic Research to Generate Questions and Adapt Other Findings

Basic research aims to answer foundational questions about how things work, like the human body or the earth's atmosphere, rather than how to change or fix those things. Relevant basic research for education leaders is often generated by researchers working in disciplines outside education, like psychology and neuroscience. "The Science of Learning," a free resource from Deans for Impact, a nonprofit group of education leaders, shows how some basic research findings translate into good practice in the classroom—even though the findings do not evaluate specific classroom practices.[7] For example, knowing that learning requires transferring information from working memory to long-term memory may not seem useful for education—but it is helpful to know that scaffolding problems through "worked examples" is a way of putting this proven finding into practice.[8]

Knowledge generated through basic research can help when you are diagnosing problems and brainstorming their potential answers. For example, neuroimaging studies found that parts of the brain look different in people with dyslexia than in others.[9] This finding, which supports the notion that dyslexia is a diagnosable condition, could help motivate practitioners to implement new screening and evaluation procedures—or policy makers to mandate screening and evaluation. This example also illustrates the limitations of basic research. Screening students for dyslexia at school requires a practical screening mechanism. And brain scans alone don't reveal what constitutes effective instruction for those students once they are identified. Similarly, the knowledge that trauma changes the brain, as studies have shown, helps you understand that some students have different needs than others do—but it won't tell you how to meet those needs.[10] In this way, basic research can be a great way to start practice—and policy—conversations, but it isn't an effective way to resolve what to do.

Basic research can also help you interpret large-scale quantitative studies of educational strategies that fall into the gray area of relevance. You may find a great research article on a strategy you want to learn more about, but the study's setting, sample, variant of strategy, or outcomes differ from yours. This example goes back to the challenge of establishing the relevance of research. How close is close enough to be informative? It depends on what you are studying and how you think it works. Basic research can help you understand how sensitive a strategy is likely to be to particular conditions, even if it hasn't been evaluated under all of them.

Qualitative Research to Get Inside the Black Box

Qualitative research can provide insight into the hows and whys often omitted from the quantitative, often causal, analyses so crucial for strong program evaluation. Like quantitative research, qualitative studies rely on systematically collected data that are thoughtfully analyzed to allow for inferences. Qualitative research analyzes narratives, stories, and perspectives rather than numerical indicators. To do this, it uses a wide range of methods of inquiry, including interviews, focus groups, ethnographies, and even historical and legal analysis.

To be sure, you can also hear plenty of stories and perspectives from media reports or from colleagues sharing their observations. But those sources might just come from the squeaky wheels. In contrast, good qualitative research takes a systematic approach. It should have a clear and well-justified data collection process, be conducted by trained and culturally sensitive field researchers, explain the implications of the findings, address limitations and alternative explanations, and assess the generalizability of the research.[11] These requirements make good qualitative research time-consuming and painstaking—but worth the effort. Consider the following scenarios.

Jim Robinson is on the school board in a large urban district with a choice-based high school system. The board wants to know how effective the choice system is at reducing the inequality that stems from the link between the neighborhood of residence and school assignment.

He finds useful research from a qualitative study of New York City public schools. The researchers learned that the majority of middle school counselors there took a passive role when it came to advising students on high school choice. The counselors believed that it was not their business to tell parents what to do, nor did they have sufficient time or support to do so. Through structured interviews with a representative sample of school counselors, the researchers learned that passive counseling limits the ability of choice policies to overcome inequality, because parents' ability to navigate the decision on their own was tightly linked to their own socioeconomic advantage.[12]

Jim takes this information to the other board members. With this newfound understanding of how the New York City counselors acted, and why, the board could more effectively work to change the counselors' practice. The board decides to adapt its strategy by establishing professional development and counseling materials that foster a more active role.

▪   ▪   ▪

Lisa Hurling is her district's curriculum director and has been unhappy with the students' results in their online credit-recovery classes. She is considering switching vendors when, at a conference, she learns about a study on this very topic. In the study, the researchers observed students who were enrolled in online credit-recovery classes. The investigators saw that many of the students were on their phones, playing games, and talking to friends instead of engaging with their online courses. There was little interaction between the students and the instructors. Even the students who were working on the online courses weren't necessarily actively involved in learning. Instead, the students were using Google and Wikipedia to search for answers to assessment questions.[13]

What she learns makes Lisa rethink how the district is monitoring the use of its system and whether the district wants an online system at all, given the implementation challenge. The findings of the study reported at the conference make her less likely to think that getting a new vendor would solve her problem.

WHAT'S NOT IN ESSA

ESSA's levels of evidence focus on whether a strategy worked—at least once, perhaps in a context irrelevant to your own. They are only about what makes research convincing, not relevant. And they don't reveal anything about a strategy's practical significance, like the feasibility of implementation or cost-effectiveness. To know what makes sense, you need to ask three types of questions—even if a strategy is supported by what ESSA deems the strongest evidence:

▪ Is the strategy designed for the problem we have diagnosed? (Have you diagnosed the problem before picking a strategy?)

- Is it feasible for us to implement this strategy?

- If so, does the evidence suggest that this strategy will produce the desired change in outcomes in a cost-effective way?

Respecting evidence doesn't mean throwing common sense out the window. Research might point to one strategy as more effective (or more cost-effective) than another, but you need to continue to rely on your professional expertise and common sense as well. If the more effective strategy is instructionally, logistically, or otherwise at odds with other aspects of your plan, that strategy doesn't make sense—no matter how effective it is.

Although ESSA points schools toward creating their own evidence through its definition of demonstrating "a rationale," the law doesn't detail how you should go about doing so. The next chapter will discuss how you can build your own evidence.

KEY TAKEAWAYS

* ESSA and other evidence-based policy emphasize research evidence that aims to answer questions about how a particular strategy *causes* an outcome.

* ESSA's requirements have nothing to say about the relevance of evidence, only its technical merits.

* ESSA deems a strategy evidence-based at the promising level if there is at least one study with a statistically significant effect on a relevant outcome and with at least one control variable to address selection bias. ESSA never requires strong or moderate evidence without permitting promising evidence as well.

* Although ESSA does not require it, be open to other forms of inquiry, including basic or pure scientific research and qualitative studies.

* ESSA encourages districts to learn from their own experiences, requiring this learning for strategies that "demonstrate a rationale."

* This chapter discusses federal requirements; if your state or district asks for more, read the policy carefully so that you can understand exactly what's required.

APPLY YOUR LEARNING

☐ Determine if the study you consulted in chapter 3 qualifies as at least promising evidence. Don't worry if you can't tell whether it is moderate or promising. What makes you classify the study as meeting that level of evidence?

☐ Have you had to change course or ignore a new strategy because what you wanted to do wasn't sufficiently evidence-based (or, to use the US Department of Education's language before ESSA, didn't have "scientifically based research" to support it)? Use the strategies in chapter 2 to look for research on these strategies. Do any studies qualify as providing at least promising evidence?

5

BUILD EVIDENCE BY LEARNING FROM YOUR OWN DATA

We have arrived at the do-it-yourself research chapter. When should you do it yourself? Ideally, you should do it all the time—even when you've seen some existing research that relates to the topic. The only way to learn from and improve your work is to study how a strategy works in your own environment. This is the central point of a Plan-Do-Study-Act cycle, continuous improvement cycles, and other models for school improvement. You should use whatever improvement process works for you and your team, but be sure to put greater emphasis on making careful comparisons than what most models require. If you're already using data for improvement, the tips in this chapter will show you how to take that work to the next level. If not, it will get you started. Either way, you'll be generating new evidence in the process.

This chapter is not technical but will use two words with their statistical, rather than common, meanings: *observations* and *variables*. If data are displayed in a table (e.g., table 5.1), each row is usually an *observation*, like a student, teacher, or school, and each column is a *variable*, like days absent, a yes-no indicator for chronic absenteeism, and a transportation variable indicating whether the student is assigned to a bus route.

Table 5.1 shows a small portion of chronic absenteeism task force chair Erin Frazier's data for one school year. The full data set would have as many rows as there are students, in all grade levels and classrooms, and would include many more than these five columns, with other columns recording the values of additional variables. But even this small excerpt of a larger data set contains too much information. You cannot just look at the whole thing and make any sense of it, so we'll need to simplify it.

TABLE 5.1

Example of student-level attendance data of kindergartners in Lincoln School District, 2018–2019				
STUDENT ID	**TEACHER**	**DAYS ABSENT**	**CHRONICALLY ABSENT**	**ASSIGNED TO BUS ROUTE**
16342	Diaz	22	Yes	No
84943	Diaz	3	No	Yes
13843	Diaz	15	No	Yes
62034	Jones	8	No	No

Turning to your data is often the best—if not the only—way of being sure that you do indeed know what you have assumed to be true. These "How do I know?" questions can sometimes be answered by looking at particular data points (e.g., which students had the lowest attendance rates?) or summary statistics (e.g., what was the average number of days absent for kindergarteners?). Answering those questions with data is a critical and often overlooked opportunity—but it's also relatively straightforward. This chapter focuses on answering more complex questions by making comparisons.

SIMPLIFY FIRST

Imagine looking at the database that table 5.1 was drawn from, with all students in the districts, across all the grades and schools. You'd be scrolling up and down, left and right, and would struggle to get the big picture, much less draw comparisons. To see the forest among the trees, simplify the data.

The *mean*, or average, of the data is a common way to do that. The data set had a value for the attendance rate for every student in the district; the mean boils all those data down to just one number: the average value across all students. When Keisha, the data manager, looked at attendance rates for elementary grades in the Lincoln School District, she found that on average, elementary students missed 6.1 percent of school days in 2018–2019.

But what if you want more nuance than just the average, but without being overwhelmed by the details for each individual student? You can look at the full spread of the data, also referred to as the distribution. The mean shows the average number of absences, but you might also want to know something about the number of absences for students who are absent relatively frequently and infrequently. Imagine lining up all the elementary students in rank order of days absent, from those absent the least (the minimum value of absences) to those absent the most (the maximum value). The student in the exact middle of the line is at the 50th percentile, also called the *median*: this student was absent 4.7 percent of school days, which was more often than 50 percent of the students. A student at the 90th percentile for absences missed 13.7 percent of days; stated differently, 90 percent of students missed less than 13.7 percent of days. The median describes what is typical. As observations at the high or low end of a distribution get more extreme, they change the mean, but not necessarily the median. In this example, those students missing more than 13.7 percent of days are lifting the mean (6.1 percent of school days missed) above the median (4.7 percent of days missed).

Another way to show the distribution of absences is to take the many values across all students (e.g., absenteeism rates of zero, 1 percent, 2 percent, 3 percent, etc.) and group them into fewer categories, such as "absent less than 5 percent of days in the school year," "absent 5 to 9.9 percent," "absent 10 to 14.9 percent," and so on, as in table 5.2. You can then display the number and percentage of students in each category.

TABLE 5.2

Absence rates for elementary students, 2018–2019		
PERCENTAGE OF DAYS ABSENT	NUMBER OF STUDENTS	PERCENTAGE OF STUDENTS
0–4.9	834	52.8
5–9.9	450	28.5
10–14.9	174	11.0
15–19.9	68	4.3
20–24.9	28	1.8
More than 25	26	1.6

Simplify, and Compare the Data with Goals

These different ways of simplifying the data don't show how good or bad what you see is. For that, you need to compare the data with a goal or benchmark—something that tells you whether what you're seeing is desirable or reasonable. In the case of chronic absenteeism, you don't expect all students to have perfect attendance, but you also don't want to see many, if any, children missing 20 percent or more of school days—that's one day out of five! If the district had previously set a goal for its chronic absenteeism rate, that might be a good comparison point. In Erin's case, she could start with comparing Lincoln's rate, 21.8 percent, with the state average, 12.9 percent.

Education leaders are often exhorted to set goals that are "ambitious but attainable" for their work. This often leads them to select a specific performance level to aim for by a set date, like 100 percent proficiency in twelve years (yes, we are talking about you, No Child Left Behind!). Evidence can provide a concrete reality check for how attainable that goal is by analyzing the rate of improvement needed to reach the goal. In the end, goal setting is a judgment call that must consider stakeholder feedback and community values. But putting evidence in the mix will help you ensure that your goals are within the realm of possible (see the sidebar "Using Data to Set Goals").

Using Data to Set Goals

To use the most basic sniff test of whether a goal is too ambitious, consider whether anyone has ever attained the rate of improvement you would need to reach your goal in the relevant time frame. A more refined approach is to think about whether districts (or schools, classrooms, or states) like yours, in whatever way seems most relevant for the problem at hand, have attained that rate of improvement (see the sidebar "Percent Change Versus Percentage Point Change" later in this chapter).You may want to look at annual improvement rates for each of the past few years and, for longer-range goals, try measures like the total change over the past three to five years.

Here are some guiding questions for conducting this type of analysis. We have focused them on setting a districtwide goal, but you could use similar questions for schools, states, or any other organizational level.

- How much improvement has your district made overall on this measure in each of the last several years? If your district has multiple schools serving similar grade levels related to the outcome, how much improvement has each school made? What is the range of improvement: the fastest and slowest rates of change?

■ How much improvement have similar districts made? Your state education agency may have published data that will help you make these comparisons.

■ If the trend has been fairly flat or getting worse overall but with some districts doing better, what has been the rate of improvement among those on the upswing? Look to those improving faster than average (e.g., in the 75th and 90th percentiles of improvement), to get a sense of how much progress the strong performers have made in the past.

■ How much improvement have similar districts made when they used strategies that research suggests are effective?

BUILD ANSWERS BY MAKING COMPARISONS

The state's letter to Superintendent Rebecca Sisti reported schoolwide rates of chronic absenteeism in her district. The letter included one set of comparisons—the rates at the different schools within the district—but the data have even more dimensions her team could use. Many of these ways of breaking down (or more formally, disaggregating) the data will be familiar from reports you have already encountered as a professional. The best approach depends on the question at hand and the data you have. Here are some general ways of breaking down data:

■ by time (e.g., school year, grading period, week)

■ by jurisdiction (e.g., state, county, district)

■ by school building

■ by grade or subject, for individual schools, districts, or states

■ by classroom (keeping in mind that a teacher in one subject could affect a student's performance in other subjects)

■ by student demographics (possibly including groups not defined in your state's accountability system)

You can also compare one outcome with another for a set group of students, schools, or districts: How do math scores compare with English language arts? Are attendance and achievement correlated?

When you have a lot of data, you have many potential comparisons. But the more separate comparisons you make—or are presented with—the further you may get from the question you set out to answer. This excessive slicing of the data into too many comparisons can lead to Death by a Thousand Tables. While you might spend only a few seconds to produce the comparisons, doing so will clog up your desktop and your mind, making it harder to focus. If you've ever looked at your state's accountability reports about your schools, you probably know what we mean. Luckily, there's a vaccine to protect against Death by a Thousand Tables: Start with your questions, and stick with them. Only make the comparisons your questions dictate.

We next describe some common types of more explicit comparisons: comparing over time; comparing outcomes for one observation (or group of observations) with other observations; and comparing one type of outcome with another. You can use these comparisons on their own or, more powerfully, in combination.

Compare Data over Time

Has the problem been getting better or worse? Over what length of time? The answers to these descriptive sorts of questions can help you think about anything else that may have been changing concurrently. Make these comparisons to start diagnosing the problem and thinking of potential strategies to address it. Erin's team, for example, might decide to track attendance rates over the past five years at each of the four elementary schools in the district (table 5.3).

It can be easier to process this kind of information visually, so in figure 5.1, we show a quick-and-dirty graph using the default formatting from Microsoft Excel. This format is good enough to show the gist of what the data are saying. In chapter 6, we will discuss how to improve the formatting for maximum clarity and impact.

A comparison over time is often from one year to the next, but it doesn't need to be. For example, Erin could also compare absenteeism rates from month to month, rather than year to year. Or she could use multiyear averages, which can be helpful if the sample is small or if absenteeism rates bounce around greatly from year to year.

Changes over time can give useful clues to what might be going on. But on their own, *changes over time don't prove cause and effect*. We've indulged in italics here because we wanted to get your attention. The world is a complicated place: one thing doesn't change while everything else stays the same. When we spoke with researchers about common misperceptions to tackle in this book, this was their number one request: be sure to emphasize that before-and-after comparisons do not prove cause and effect.

TABLE 5.3

	Chronic absenteeism by elementary school and year			
	PERCENTAGE OF STUDENTS			
SCHOOL YEAR	Hillside	Lemont	King	White Oak
2014–15	13.5	13.8	8.4	9.6
2015–16	15.2	12.1	10.6	12.3
2016–17	14.7	11.7	10.4	9.8
2017–18	15.6	12.9	10.5	10.3
2018–19	17.8	16.2	12.1	10.9

FIGURE 5.1

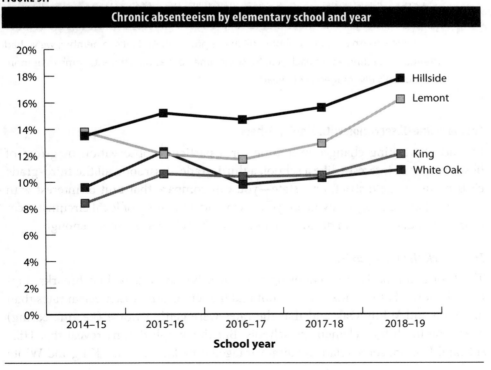

Chronic absenteeism by elementary school and year

But changes in outcomes over time can spark useful new questions, even if they don't prove that one thing caused something else. For example, did Mississippi's fourth-grade reading scores improve on the National Assessment of Education Progress from 2017 to 2019 because of professional development around reading, literacy requirements for promotion to fourth grade, or increased use of teacher coaching? Just looking at two years of data can't tell us how to allocate credit for the improvement across these strategies—or if the improvement is a statistical blip. But it does raise some fascinating possibilities that merit further study.

> Hillside Elementary School had implemented its doorway greetings strategy beginning in the fall of 2018. Principal Dennis Bollinger hadn't examined any concurrent changes in attendance or chronic absenteeism, because he and his staff weren't looking for them: they had tried the strategy in hopes of improving school climate. When they did compare their school-level rates for 2017–2018 to 2018–2019, they were disappointed: chronic absenteeism had actually increased while they implemented the greetings.
>
> Dennis spoke at the faculty meeting. "We've been happy with the greetings," he said. "They didn't cost anything, and people felt like the additional time was really mini-mal and worth the better vibes they felt in the classroom. Just because this didn't move attendance doesn't mean we should ditch the program. And let's remember, we've had attendance getting worse each year for some time now, as our students come to us more and more disadvantaged every year."

Compare One Observation with Similar Others

Instead of tracking changes over time for a particular observation or group of observations of interest—like a school, a third-grade classroom, all the third-grade classrooms in the district, or a state—you can compare that unit of interest with other similar units. By drawing on your own understanding of local circumstances or from the data, you can decide what makes other elements similar enough.

Handpick the Comparison

Think of a comparison as choosing your own benchmark or benchmarks. Figure 5.1 shows that Hillside and Lemont had higher chronic absenteeism rates than did King and White Oak and that the rates were getting worse (i.e., increasing) over time in all four elementary schools. But this graph doesn't reveal that Hillside and Lemont serve relatively disadvantaged populations while King and White

Oak serve a more advantaged group of students, so not all these comparisons are equally informative. Indeed, Amy Whyte, the principal at Lemont, doesn't think she's likely to learn anything from what's going on at King or White Oak. "All the research shows it," she says. "Poverty is bad for students, in every way. I don't want to discourage my teachers by making it seem like they've failed because they haven't been able to overcome all these disadvantages."

Comparing outcomes for one district or school with those of others serving similar students can be particularly illuminating. It's a great way to command attention and spur action. When people see better outcomes in settings similar to their own, it makes success seem possible—and could suggest who might have strategies worth learning about. In contrast, learning that schools or districts with substantially more resources or more privileged students do better is useful for documenting problems but is less actionable and can be disheartening. Comparing your own outcomes with a statewide average can unintentionally have the same effect.

You can also compare one student group with another—and not just those on your state accountability reports. Erin, for instance, asked the data manager, Keisha Marks, to present the team with information about how chronic absenteeism varied across the student characteristics mapping to the team's different hypotheses. Keisha sent Erin a table with information on how chronic absenteeism in Lincoln's elementary schools was related to whether students were assigned to a bus route (see table 5.4). Bus ridership depends on how far from school their home address is. The table shows that 13.6 percent of the students who walk to school are chronically absent, compared with the 10.6 percent who take the bus, suggesting that the students' mode of transportation might have a relationship with attendance rates.

TABLE 5.4

Chronic absenteeism by transportation to school for elementary students in Lincoln School District						
	WALKERS		BUS RIDERS		TOTAL	
STUDENT ATTENDANCE	*N*	*%*	*N*	*%*	*N*	*%*
Not chronically absent	418	86.4	1,034	89.4	1,452	88.5
Chronically absent	66	13.6	122	10.6	188	11.5
All students	484	29.5	1,156	70.5	1,640	100.0

Let the Data Pick the Comparison

Choosing your own benchmark can mean missing out on potentially better comparisons. For example, Dennis, the principal at Hillside, knows that Lemont is a relevant benchmark for his school, but he is less likely to know about elementary schools in Lundville, a district in a similar metropolitan region on the other side of the state. Lundville's schools are even more demographically similar to Hillside than Lemont is.

A state education agency could be helpful in facilitating these more systematic comparisons across schools or districts. For example, the Massachusetts Department of Elementary and Secondary Education's District Analysis and Review Tool suggests comparable districts according to grade span, enrollment, and composition of students in special populations.[1] Or a large district could help make these comparisons for individual schools whose leaders may not know each other. If your state or district does not help with this matchmaking, you can always turn to publicly available data on state and federal websites.

It's oversimplifying to say, "Let the data pick the comparisons," though, because a human must decide what makes units comparable. And that depends on what type of question you are asking. Consider these examples:

- Are you trying to diagnose a school's role in a problem? You might want to compare its outcomes with those of schools that have similar demographic profiles, to account for the effects of structural forces outside education (e.g., a high concentration of poverty at the school).[2]

- Are you trying to evaluate the impact of a particular instructional strategy? You might find it more useful to compare your outcomes with those schools similar to yours in terms of their other instructional strategies or resource levels, rather than looking at demographically similar schools. The idea is to find out what would have happened if you had not implemented your strategy.

Imagine that Dennis knows that the Lundville elementary schools are a near-perfect demographic match for Hillside, even more so than Lemont is. Further, let's say he knows that none of the Lundville schools used the greetings strategy. Would comparing chronic absenteeism rates at Hillside to those in the Lundville schools prove anything about the effectiveness of the greetings strategy? Probably not. Just as comparisons over time can be complicated by other contemporaneous changes, comparisons between schools can be complicated by other differences between the schools. In this case, he would want to know why Hillside was implementing door-way greetings and why Lundville was not. Did Dennis and his staff care more about school climate or pay more attention to research than did the staff in Lundville? If so, they might implement other practices (like trying out other ideas the Hillside staff got from Edutopia) that could be responsible for any observed disparities in chronic absenteeism. The use of the greetings strategy just happens to be a differ-ence Dennis and his team know about. Or it could go in the other direction: maybe the team at Hillside cared about school climate because they had observed some newly emerging problems with it, while things in Lundville seemed to be improv-ing. So Hillside could look worse than Lundville in terms of chronic absenteeism, but this status might be despite the greetings rather than because of them.

Even if the greetings did nothing, there are many potential explanations for the pattern we see in the data. Any time you want to evaluate the impact of a strategy, ask why one group participated and another one didn't. Could those reasons (dif-ferences in leadership, capacity, or other considerations that you might not be able to measure but that seem logical) be responsible for the outcome you are tracking, rather than the strategy you want to learn about?

Combine Comparisons

Combining comparisons helps combat the real-world problem of multiple factors usually changing at the same time. The best way to combine comparisons depends on the selection bias you're worried about—and, of course, the data you can access.

> As math department head at a large urban middle school, Maria Gonzalez wants to eval-uate the impact of the eighth-grade math reteaching strategy. Her goal is to improve her school's average scaled scores on the state's eighth-grade math test to at least as high as the school's average scaled score in seventh-grade math.[3] One way to do this is to compare the difference in state test scores between seventh and eighth grades in 2019 (when the eighth graders experienced the reteaching strategy) with the same difference in 2018 (before the strategy was implemented). This approach has an intuitive appeal because most of the eighth graders in 2019 were seventh graders in 2018. Roughly speaking, Maria is comparing the same students' performance over time. (This is less true in schools with high rates of student mobility or retention in grade. For example, in a school or district with high dropout rates, a ninth-grade cohort in one year may differ substantially and systematically from those who are in twelfth grade three years later.)

Table 5.5 shows the results Maria needs to make these comparisons using what's called a difference-in-differences analysis.

Let's dig into this table. The average scaled scores are in cells A (seventh grade 2018), B (eighth grade 2018), C (seventh grade 2019), and D (eighth grade 2019). All the other cells in the table are calculated from those four averages.

What got Maria worried about the eighth-grade test scores in the first place was the gap in seventh- and eighth-grade scores. Cell E shows that in 2018—*before* the reteaching strategy—the difference between the eighth-grade score of 232.3 and the seventh-grade score of 240.1 is −7.8. After the team implements the reteaching strategy in eighth grade in 2019, the eighth graders' scores improve to 237.8, a difference of 5.5 scaled score points (cell H).

Why not stop there with the analysis? As we stressed earlier, you must resist the common belief that changes over time prove cause and effect. Just because the eighth graders did better the year that reteaching was initiated does not mean that the reteaching is what caused the improvement. Perhaps the eighth graders are doing better in 2019 because of schoolwide changes unrelated to the new eighth-grade reteaching strategy—changes that would affect all students in the school, including seventh and eighth graders alike. Maria may not be able to measure those changes (e.g., a change in school climate), and she may not even be aware that some small shifts are happening. But she can still try to account for them, through smart

TABLE 5.5

Difference-in-differences analysis to compare trends in seventh- and eighth-grade average scaled scores on the state mathematics test			
	SEVENTH-GRADE MATHEMATICS SCALED SCORE	EIGHTH-GRADE MATHEMATICS SCALED SCORE	DIFFERENCE BETWEEN EIGHTH GRADE AND SEVENTH GRADE
2018 (pre-strategy)	240.1 (A)	232.3 (B)	−7.8 (E = B − A)
2019 (post-strategy)	242.4 (C)	237.8 (D)	−4.6 (F = D − C)
Difference between 2019 and 2018	+2.3 (G = C − A)	+5.5 (H = D − B)	+3.2 (F − E) or (H − G) (difference in differences)

choices about her comparisons. The difference-in-differences idea is to look at what happened to seventh graders from 2018 to 2019—their scaled scores improved a bit, by 2.3 scaled score points (cell G)—and use it as a proxy for how much we would expect eighth-grade scores to have changed from 2018 to 2019 *if there had been no change in math instruction.*

Overall, the eighth graders improved by 5.5 points between 2018 and 2019. We can think of this 5.5 point increase as the net effect of the reteaching impact *plus* all the stuff we don't know about schoolwide. The seventh graders improved by 2.3 points. For this approach to work, we need to think that this 2.3 point increase is a good measure of all the schoolwide stuff we don't observe. The *difference in the differences* is 3.2 points. The difference in differences is a better estimate of the potential impact of the reteaching strategy than is a comparison of the eighth-grade trend over time, because the difference in the differences also accounts for what might have happened even if the team hadn't implemented reteaching.

Alternatively, we can think of the difference-in-differences estimate as measuring how the gap between seventh- and eighth-grade scores changed from 2018 (cell E) to 2019 (cell F). Either set of calculations (F − E or H − G) will yield the identical estimate of +3.2 points.

Before interpreting this estimate as showing cause and effect, though, Maria needs to think about whether anything else important was going on at the same time and could explain her results. The preceding analysis assumes that nothing other than the math strategy was changing for seventh and eighth graders at the school between 2018 and 2019. But what if the school had first implemented a new behavioral program for eighth graders, but not seventh graders, in 2019? One way to help get around anything that might confound the results would be to consider changes in a different outcome that she thinks would not be affected by the math changes but would be affected by the new behavioral program in a similar way that math scores might be affected. Maria could compare changes in eighth-grade math scaled scores with eighth-grade English language arts (ELA) scaled scores, as shown in table 5.6.

In this case, the eighth graders are doing a little better in ELA than in math overall: a difference of 7.5 scaled score points in 2018. Their math scores improved by 5.5 points between 2018 and 2019, as compared to 1.2 points for ELA. So, they gained 4.3 *more* points on math than they did on ELA. She can make a good argument that this difference in the differences is *because* of the reteaching strategy because, unlike the behavioral program, the reteaching strategy affected only math and not ELA.

TABLE 5.6

Difference in differences to compare trends between eighth-grade English language arts (ELA) and eighth-grade mathematics scaled scores on the state test			
	ELA SCALED SCORE	MATHEMATICS SCALED SCORE	DIFFERENCE BETWEEN MATHEMATICS AND ELA SCORES
2018 (pre-strategy)	239.8	232.3	−7.5
2019 (post-strategy)	241.0	237.8	−3.2
Difference between 2019 and 2018	+1.2	+5.5	+4.3

We've just shown you the intuition and basic calculations behind what's known as *difference in differences*, one of the most common forms of combining comparisons. Academic researchers who use this technique do additional, technically fancy stuff that we don't cover here, but the basic idea holds: there is information to be found in comparing a change over time with a change for a relevant comparison group. This approach is useful for answering many types of questions, so it's a good one to have in your toolkit.

Let's walk through another example, this time with Keisha, the data manager who Erin asked to estimate the impact of the greetings strategy at Hillside Elementary School on attendance rates. Keisha knows that the student body at both schools was becoming poorer each year. So if she only compares Hillside's attendance rates from 2017–2018 to 2018–2019, it won't account for the liklihood that Hillside's students were likely to attend school less frequently in 2018–2019 anyhow, because of the changing student population.

Another option is comparing Hillside with Lemont Elementary School. But simply comparing Hillside's attendance rate with Lemont's in 2018–2019, after the greetings strategy was in place, wasn't satisfying, either. This method would bundle together the differences between the two schools' use (or nonuse) of a greetings strategy with any other differences between the schools that year, including organizational, leadership, or demographic dissimilarities. But combining a comparison over time with a comparison between the schools helps address any sneaking suspicions that things other than the strategy of interest also differ over time or between schools.

Table 5.7 combines comparisons over time and schools. The bottom row of the table shows that although chronic absenteeism at Hillside went up 2.2 percentage points, from 15.6 percent to 17.8 percent between 2017–2018 and 2018–2019, it went up even more, by 3.3 percentage points, at Lemont during that period. This gap is even greater when we think in terms of percentage change, rather than percentage point change (see the sidebar "Percent Change Versus Percentage Point Change").

As we saw in figure 5.1, chronic absenteeism was increasing over time in general in the district—so we don't want to consider the increase as part of the effect of the greetings at Hillside. The bottom right cell in table 5.7 shows the difference-in-differences estimate. This estimate compares the differences over time at the two schools (2.2 percentage points at Hillside minus 3.3 percentage points at Lemont). The difference in differences is a way of subtracting out the general increase over time (that is, what happened at the Lemont school) so that all that is left is the difference due to whatever changed differently at Hillside versus Lemont between the two years. For this approach to be convincing, you must know what else might have been happening over this period. If the greetings strategy was the main school-specific change at either school during this time, then it's reasonable to attribute the difference-in-differences estimate to the greetings.

TABLE 5.7

Difference in differences to compare trends in chronic absenteeism rates at Hillside and Lemont Elementary Schools			
	HILLSIDE	**LEMONT**	**DIFFERENCE BETWEEN LEMONT AND HILLSIDE**
2017–18 (pre-strategy) absenteeism rate	15.6%	12.9%	−2.7 ppts
2018–19 (post-strategy) absenteeism rate	17.8%	16.2%	−1.6 ppts
Difference between 2018–19 and 2017–18	+2.2 ppts	+3.3 ppts	+1.1 ppts

Note: ppts = percentage points.

Percent Change Versus Percentage Point Change

Here's how chronic absenteeism rates look in Hillside and Lemont over the last two years:

	HILLSIDE	LEMONT
2017–18 chronic absenteeism rate	15.6%	12.9%
2018–19 chronic absenteeism rate	17.8%	16.2%
Percentage point change	17.8% − 15.6% = +2.2 ppts	16.2% − 12.9% = +3.3 ppts
Percent change	(2.2/15.6) × 100 = +14.1%	(3.3/12.9) × 100 = +25.6%

As most students at Hillside or Lemont could tell you, 17.8 percent is greater than 15.6 percent—but how much greater? The difference is 17.8 minus 15.6, or 2.2 percentage points. Both 17.8 and 15.6 are reported as percentages, out of 100. To put this into a sentence (always a great test of understanding!), we can say that for each hundred students at Hillside, there were 2.2 more students chronically absent in 2018–2019 than there were in 2017–2018. This difference is a *percentage point change*: one percentage subtracted directly from another.

You might look at the third row of this table and think that the increases are pretty similar: 2.2 more students per 100 were chronically absent at Hillside than the previous year, and 3.3 more students per hundred were chronically absent at Lemont in 2018–2019 than in 2017–2018. But because the baseline chronic absenteeism rates, in 2017–2018, were different between the two schools, the difference is dramatic in percent change terms.

To calculate a *percent change*, the formula is as follows:

$$(\text{new number} - \text{old number}) \times 100$$

As Charles Wheelan puts it in his excellent general-audience introduction to statistics, *Naked Statistics*, "the numerator (the part on the top of the fraction) gives us the size of the change in absolute terms; the denominator (the part on the bottom of the fraction) is what puts this change in context by comparing it with our starting point."*

Here's an example: Hillside started at a 15.6 percent chronic absenteeism rate and increased by 2.2 percentage points to 17.8 percent. Compared with Hillside's baseline of 15.6 percent (the "old number" in the previous equation), this 2.2 percentage point increase is an overall increase of 14.1 percent. (calculated as [(17.8 − 15.6) / 15.6] × 100 = 14.1). Lemont started at 12.9 percent and increased to 16.2 percent. That's a 25.6 percent increase:

$$(16.2 - 12.9) \times 100 = 25.6$$

In other words, chronic absenteeism increased by 14.1 percent at Hillside and by 25.6 percent at Lemont. This difference is why the line for Lemont is steeper than for Hillside between 2017–2018 and 2018–2019 in figure 5.1: chronic absenteeism is increasing faster at Lemont than it is at Hillside.

Which statistic you use—percent change or percentage point change—depends on what you want to know. A percent increase is a way of thinking about a change relative to something else, while a percentage point increase is an absolute change. An increase of 1 percentage point is a much bigger deal if you're starting out low, say, at 4 percent (1/4 = 0.25, or a 25 percent increase) than if you were starting out at 50 percent (1/50 = 0.02, or a 2 percent increase).

*Charles Wheelan, *Naked Statistics: Stripping the Dread from the Data* (New York: W.W. Norton & Company, 2013).

Another way to arrive at the difference-in-differences estimate, and to conceptualize the comparison, is to think about the column on the right in table 5.7. In 2017–2018, Hillside's chronic absenteeism rate was 2.7 percentage points higher than Lemont's; by 2018–2019, the difference had shrunk to 1.6 percentage points. Again, for this approach to make sense, you need to believe that there's no other explanation for the narrowing of the gap. For example, if a large number of the Lemont students with high attendance had switched to a charter school in 2018–2019, they wouldn't count in Lemont's numbers anymore—and this departure could drive up Lemont's chronic absenteeism rate even if nothing else had changed. In that case, Lemont in 2018–2019 wouldn't be a good comparison for Lemont in 2017–2018, much less for Hillside in 2018–2019. Overall, this combination of comparisons provides more persuasive evidence for evaluating the impact of a strategy than does either comparison on its own.

Compare Many Data Points: Scatterplots and Regression Analysis

Erin is wondering how her district might anticipate which students will need more support with attendance. Could she predict which students will be chronically absent in one year by looking at which students were frequently absent the previous year? In other words, she wants to compare two variables—attendance rates in two years—for all students, rather than comparing groups of students, like kindergarteners versus first graders, or boys versus girls. Because the school year has just started, she asks Keisha to

> compare students' attendance rates for the previous two years (2017–2018 and 2018–2019), for all students who were enrolled in the school in both years. This sample leaves out most current kindergartners in the fall of 2019, because they wouldn't have been enrolled in school in 2018–2019, but the sample should be good enough to see the general pattern.

Keisha could make a table for this request, but because attendance rates can take on so many values, she would have to simplify the data first, perhaps creating categories of values (as in table 5.2, but with many more rows). But there's another option for when you want to see the relationship between two variables that can take on many values: the scatterplot, a great quick visual aid.

Keisha uses Excel to prepare the figure. She selects her data and clicks on Insert Chart > X Y (Scatter) to produce a scatterplot (figure 5.2). The horizontal axis shows the percentage of each student's days missed in 2017–2018, and the vertical axis shows the student's percentage for 2018–2019. Each student is represented by a single point. For example, one student, Carlos, who is labeled on the plot, missed 20 percent of school days in 2017–2018 and 6 percent in 2018–2019. Where many students have similar values, their points will bunch together or overlap. The horizontal and vertical lines in this figure reflect the cutoff points for the absenteeism categories in table 5.2. While table 5.2 accurately reports that 26 students missed at least 25 percent of school days in 2018–2019, the scatterplot presents more information, including the maximum value (34 percent). The scatterplot also shows in a more striking way just how far from the norm these students with the highest absenteeism rates are.

The dots show a pattern, with higher percentages of days missed in 2017–2018 corresponding to more days missed in 2018–2019. Keisha clicks again to insert a trend line, and a best-fit line appears (figure 5.3). With remarkable ease, Keisha has just estimated a linear regression. If you want to do this yourself in Excel, under Chart Tools, select Design > Add Chart > Element > Trendline > Linear. This best-fit (regression) line is the best prediction of what percentage of days students will miss in 2018–2019, in light of their attendance in 2017–2018. When the two variables have no strong relationship, the line will be flat. When the line slopes up (meaning lower on the left and higher on the right), the variables are positively related: they go up or down together. When it slopes down (again, think from left to right), they are negatively related: when one rises, the other falls. The steeper the line, the stronger the relationship.

FIGURE 5.2

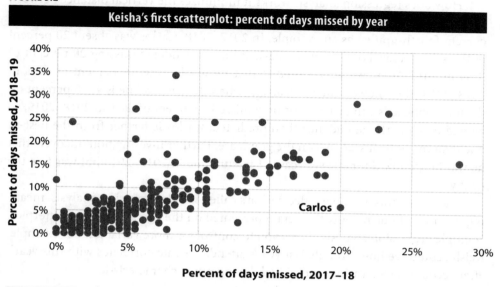

Keisha's first scatterplot: percent of days missed by year

FIGURE 5.3

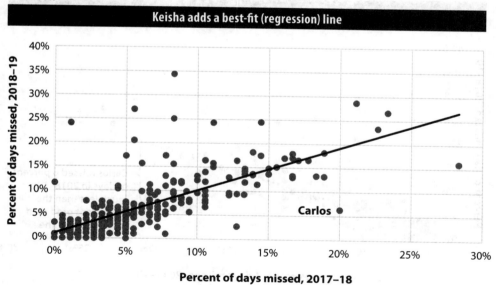

Keisha adds a best-fit (regression) line

How does regression analysis work? It minimizes the vertical distance between the best-fit line and each data point. Figure 5.4 shows this process using Carlos, a current fourth-grader, as an example. In 2017–2018, Carlos was absent 20 percent of the school year. Looking at the dashed line for students missing 20 percent of days in 2017–2018, we would predict that he would miss 19 percent of days in 2018–2019 (the value on the vertical axis when the dashed line is at 20 percent on the horizontal axis). In fact, Carlos only missed 6 percent of days in 2018–2019, so he had much better attendance than predicted. Carlos is farther from the best-fit line than the bulk of students on the graph are. Further investigation uncovers that he was hospitalized for a severe case of pneumonia in 2017–2018 but was fine the next year.

The line in this example reflects what's called *simple* regression analysis, meaning the line is fit using only the data represented on the axes of the scatterplot. Multiple-regression analysis allows you to control for more variables. For example, Keisha could see how strongly last year's attendance rate correlates with this year's after accounting for various individual demographic characteristics.

FIGURE 5.4

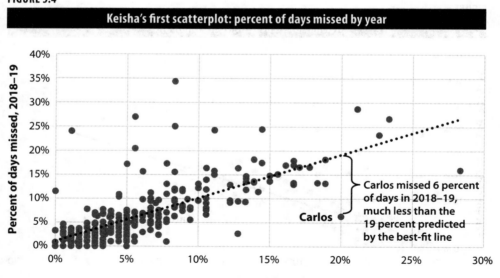

Keisha's first scatterplot: percent of days missed by year

Look to Outliers to Learn from Extreme Comparisons

Unusual or extreme data, which researchers call *outliers*, can yield insights about what is driving success or failure. An outlier can be a positive or a negative: for example, a school can have much lower rates of chronic absenteeism, or much higher, than you would expect. You can look for outlier students, teachers, schools, or districts.

Understanding the causes of outliers often involves looking at information beyond what you have available in your data systems. For example, Carlos's teacher from last year would probably remember that he had had pneumonia, and the teacher would probably share this information. As a result, this step can be more time-intensive than some other types of comparisons.

> Erin notices that several students in the upper right portion of figure 5.3 are missing much more school than others are missing—over 15 percent of school days in both school years. She decides to follow up with those classroom teachers to learn more. She also sees many students with near-perfect attendance (those near the bottom left corner of the scatterplot). Curious about what is helping these students do so well, she asks Keisha for some data on students missing fewer than five days per year. The data are not very helpful, though. These students are more likely to be white, less likely to be eligible for free or reduced-price lunch, and more likely to be placed in gifted enrichment classes than are their peers.

The scatterplot in figure 5.3 looks at two years' worth of outcomes and can show which students have particularly good or bad outcomes in either year. But if you consider data on student (or school or district) characteristics alongside outcomes, regression analysis can allow you to identify those who are excelling despite characteristics that typically predict much weaker outcomes. These are especially useful types of outliers to investigate. See, for example, a recent analysis of California school districts that are "beating the odds."[4] You can look for outliers without a graph by checking observations at or near the maximum (say, greater than the 95th or 98th percentile) and the minimum (e.g., less than the 5th or 1st percentile) values for the variable of interest.

Sometimes, looking closely at outliers can provide insight on how others might achieve good results (or avoid bad ones), but you also need to investigate carefully to avoid drawing false conclusions. Bear with us for a short, absurd example. Imagine you identify the five high schools in your state with the highest graduation rates. You decide to learn more about these schools to distill lessons for other high schools. But right away, you notice that all five schools have names that start with a C. Should you go tell all your districts to rename their high schools? Obviously not. Remember, you only looked at the five schools with the highest graduation rates. Your state probably has plenty of high schools that both start with a C and have low graduation rates. But because you are only looking at those outliers, you aren't paying any attention to the other schools. If you really wanted to learn about the relationship between starting with a C and graduation rates, you would want to look at the graduation rates for all schools beginning with a C, not just those with the best results.

While our absurd example makes the problem obvious, it's easy to get tripped up on this practice in the real world. In fact, Erin is at risk of doing the same thing by looking into just the students with the very highest and lowest absenteeism rates. When she follows up with classroom teachers, she should be sure to find out about the issues affecting *all* students and how these factors might relate to attendance. You never know when other students may be experiencing the same problems as the students with the worst attendance but are still not becoming chronically absent.

SPECIAL ISSUES WITH SOME DATA

The approach we describe in this chapter of using comparisons to answer questions works for all sorts of data sources. But assessment data and survey data pose a few special issues that are worth knowing about if you are using them.

Assessment Data

State and local assessments provide some of the most commonly used data in education. Federal law requires every student to be tested annually in ELA and mathematics in grades 3 through 8, plus once again in high school. And districts administer other assessments for purposes of placement and measuring student progress. But standardized tests—even ones that involve performance tasks, essays, and other items that are more subjective than simple multiple-choice questions—measure only a subset of what we want students to know and be able to do. This drawback is partly because some subjects and skills don't lend themselves to standardized testing formats and partly because tests need to be kept to a reasonable length—not everything can be included every year. And assessment results are often whittled down to summary statistics like percent proficient, masking a great deal of complexity that can affect what those numbers actually mean.

Scores from standardized tests fall into two categories: *norm-referenced*, in which students' scores are compared with one another (often as a percentile), and *criterion-referenced*, in which scores are compared with a level of performance (often "proficiency," "meeting expectations," or "on grade level"). Either way, student performance is often reported as a scaled score rather than percent correct. The scaling addresses the problem of variability in tests' difficulty from year to year if the items on a test change. If they get harder, students' percent correct could drop even if their underlying knowledge and skills were the same. Scaled scores attempt to account for such differences in difficulty across years.

Scaled scores are generally meant to be comparable for the same test over time, like comparing last year's and this year's scores on the grade 3 reading test. Some scaled scores are also comparable across grades or subjects within the same year, but many are not—even if the range of possible scaled score values on each test is the same.

On criterion-referenced tests, scaled scores are often broken into performance levels that describe how much a student knows and can demonstrate at a given moment (e.g., advanced, proficient, needs improvement). Some assessments also provide growth scores, which measure how much a student has learned or gained since a previous test. Growth scores can only be provided for students who have scores available from at least one previous test.

People often measure school improvement by comparing changes in a school's percentage of students proficient over time, but such an approach is fraught with problems. The rate of change in percent proficient depends on how many students are close to the proficient cutoff point on that test. If many are near the cutoff, more students will move across the proficient/not-proficient line from one year to the next than if most are performing farther away from the cutoff point. It's much easier to show progress on percent proficient when you have many students near proficiency—but that doesn't mean that other schools aren't improving just as quickly. For more on this, see Leah Shafer's article "When Proficient Isn't Good," from *Usable Knowledge*.[5]

What to do instead? You can compare average scaled scores, not percent proficient, across schools. Doing so will show you the differences in school performance for the average student in the school. Or if you're particularly interested in the trend for the lowest performing students rather than the average student, you could compare the scaled score at, say, the 10th percentile. This would tell you the difference in school performance for the students at the 10th percentile in each school. If you really want to stick with percentages, look at the change in the percentages of students in each performance category, for example, the percentage who scored "advanced" and "needs improvement" along with the percentage who scored "proficient."

Here are some recommendations for using assessment data smartly:

- Be sure you know which topics are covered on a test so that you are not using it to monitor something the test wasn't intended to measure.

- Carefully read the guidance on interpreting a test's scores to find out which comparisons are valid and which are not—even when scores are reported on the same scale.

- To measure school improvement, compare average scaled scores over time and compare progress along the full distribution of scores, not just at proficiency.

The book *Data Wise: A Step-by-Step Guide to Using Assessment Results to Improve Teaching and Learning* covers the use of assessment data in greater detail if you'd like to learn more.[6]

Survey Data

Surveys are tempting means of data collection, especially for popular concepts that, like school climate and student engagement, don't map cleanly to variables in administrative data sets. Free tools like Google Forms make surveys easy to distribute and respond to. Response data come in analysis-ready format (except for open-ended text responses, which require more work). And they are an easy way to show that you asked for input in tasks requiring "stakeholder engagement." But this ease of collection also comes with risks.

Survey research is a specialized field. Many aspects of survey design are not obvious and can lead to problems. If you're going to do a big survey, you should seek help from a survey expert. Here are some parts of the survey that seem straightforward but actually aren't.[7]

- *How you write each question:* The wording of questions matters in many ways, but a good guiding principle is to write questions that are both simple and specific. The Pew Research Center offers helpful advice on questionnaire design.[8]

- *How you list multiple-choice answers:* The full set of choices you offer affects how people respond. And anchoring bias makes respondents give the first option listed special weight in their minds. They interpret subsequent options relative to it.

- *The order of the questions:* Earlier questions may plant seeds that stay with respondents as they move on to later questions, making particular responses to the first questions more salient. Respondents may also distort their responses in an attempt to remain consistent across questions.

- *Using surveys to capture socioemotional measures for accountability purposes:* Heed the caution of psychology professors Angela Duckworth and David Yeager, who write, "We do not believe any available measure is suitable for between-school accountability judgments."[9]

When you get results back from your survey, even if your questions are expertly constructed, don't expect the respondents to be highly representative of the population of interest. This is especially true if the survey is opt-in or has low responses rates for other reasons.

MAKE YOUR OWN RESEARCH RELEVANT AND CONVINCING TOO

Whatever form do-it-yourself research takes, you need to ask the same questions of your own work that you would ask of someone else's. Doing it yourself gives you a huge head start on relevance; the harder part is ensuring that you've convinced yourself of your findings. In chapter 6, we'll explain how to communicate those convincing results to your audience.

KEY TAKEAWAYS

* To build evidence from your own data, start with your questions. Refer to chapter 1 for help coming up with questions that diagnose problems, assess the implementation of a strategy, and evaluate its impact.

* Simplify your data to see the forest from the trees. Consider the whole distribution of a variable, not just the middle (average).

* Structure comparisons to answer your question, holding potentially complicating factors constant where you can. You can compare time frames, schools, or groups—or best of all, try mixing and matching your comparisons.

* Graph your data with scatterplots to see the big picture.

* Use regression analysis to see how two variables move together when other variables are held constant.

* Interpret your findings with the same standards you apply to judge how relevant and convincing others' research is. By definition the findings should be quite relevant (see chapter 3). In particular, ask these questions:

  • Is one thing likely to have caused another? How do you know that the comparison at hand is responsible? Think hard about all the possible causes of the differences.

  • How do you know if something is due to chance? Do you care?

  • How do you know if something is cost-effective? Gather more information as needed.

APPLY YOUR LEARNING

☐ Choose a question that requires you to go to your own data. (For these quantitative data questions, we recommend a question about diagnosing a problem or evaluating impact rather than implementation.)

☐ What data will you use to answer the question? What system stores these data? Will you work with the data yourself, or if not, whom will you ask to do so?

☐ Which variables interest you? Which measures in the data set map to the concepts you care about? How strongly do these measures match the concepts? If your best option is relatively weak, you can still move forward, but you need to interpret your results with this shortcoming in mind.

☐ Which observations do you want to consider in your analysis? For example, will you be considering all third-grade students or all the students in a particular school or classroom? All algebra teachers? In which years?

☐ Does your question relate to the average (mean), the median, the students doing unusually poorly or well, or other measures from the full distribution for your question? How will this decision affect your analysis plan?

☐ Are you attempting to answer a question of cause and effect? If so, what comparisons will convince you? What other explanations will you need to rule out?

☐ Imagine that you have a data manager at your disposal. Write this person a short email describing what you want to know. Try to include enough detail so that the manager could complete the analysis with just this information alone.

6

INTERPRET AND SHARE YOUR EVIDENCE

It's early November, and Superintendent Rebecca Sisti and the absenteeism task force are meeting again to review the evidence they have gathered so far.

"I was disappointed at first to see that Hillside's chronic absenteeism rate was the highest for elementary schools last year," says Principal Dennis Bollinger. "But now that I know that Lemont's rate increased much faster than ours last year, it looks like things might have been even worse if we hadn't started the doorway greetings."

"I agree," says Rebecca. "It seems like a simple thing we could do right away, while we also work on developing our longer-term strategy to improve attendance. We can show pretty good evidence that it worked here in Lincoln."

"Well, it worked in an elementary school," says Erin Frazier, the task force chair. "My bet is that the elementary teachers will be on board. But the middle school teachers might be a tougher sell."

The task force discusses the evidence further and decides to recommend that every classroom teacher in the elementary schools, and every homeroom teacher in the middle school, should greet every student personally every day, starting right after the December break. The task force will continue to meet to come up with a more in-depth plan for improving attendance across all Lincoln's schools, but the greetings strategy will at least get something up and running while the members finish their research.

"We'll need to think carefully about how to share what we've learned in a way that will convince everyone this is worth doing," says Rebecca. "Let's talk about how we can do that at the all-district professional development day coming up in a couple of weeks."

Chapter 1 described how to begin the inquiry process by defining a problem. You then learned how to turn that problem into questions that evidence can help answer, how to find evidence quickly, how to decide if that evidence is relevant and convincing, and how to build an answer with your own data. By now you have collected lots of evidence and are homing in on answers. But solving a problem requires more than knowing what the evidence says. It also requires interpreting the evidence so that people can understand it and can act.

Interpretation helps your audience understand your data and draw out its implications. By showing your audience how you know that your findings and interpretation are accurate, you make it easier for them to believe these as well. We will show you how to use examples, words, and visuals to direct your audience's attention to the findings that matter most and how to put your results in a scale and context that will resonate with your audience.

This chapter will focus on Rebecca Sisti, who wants all her elementary and middle school teachers to implement Hillside's greetings strategy and to provide additional support for teachers with particularly disruptive classrooms. She plans to use the next district professional development day to share the research she has discovered and Erin's analysis of the Lincoln School District data. What pieces of evidence are most relevant to convincing her teachers to make this change, and how can Rebecca present those findings most persuasively? That is, how can she share her answer to the question "How do I know?"

IDENTIFY THE MOST POWERFUL EVIDENCE

After all your work looking for existing research and building your own evidence, you probably have quite a bit of information at your fingertips. If you're like us, you may be tempted to include as much of that information as you can, to justify the work that went into creating it or to show all the data that reinforces your conclusion. But such a data-heavy approach is missing the point. Your job is not to make your audience go through the same process you did but to show them the simplest path from evidence to action. You need to leave out all the wrong turns and switchbacks you took along the way. Even more important, you need to prioritize the evidence that is most likely to inspire the action you seek.

You have already done some of this work by narrowing down the questions you answered in the first place, using the tools we shared earlier to avoid your own Death by a Thousand Tables. But you will probably need to do more work to make your evidence simple and clear to all. Which evidence to keep, which to refine, and which to drop depends on your audience and your goal.

Five Questions for Selecting the Evidence Your Audience Needs

Rebecca wants her elementary and middle school teachers to implement Hillside's greetings strategy—in the main classrooms for elementary students and in home-rooms for middle school students. But these two groups of teachers are coming from different perspectives. She expects that most of her elementary school teachers will be supportive of this strategy, though they will still want to understand why they should make this change and what it will mean for them and their students. She anticipates that her middle school teachers, who she knows feel more strapped for time, will be less initially supportive and will take more convincing.

Rebecca needs to decide what evidence she'll need to convince these two groups to adopt the strategy. The evidence could come from the analyses Erin conducted or from other research she has uncovered. To narrow down the possibilities, she asks herself five key questions about her audience members:

- *What do they already know?* What baseline knowledge can she count on everyone's having? As an educator, you know that starting from existing knowledge to build new knowledge is an effective teaching strategy; you can use the same principle here. Rebecca believes that most people will be attuned to the data around average daily attendance and will know that absenteeism counts in the school accountability system this year.

- *What do the audience members think they know but really don't?* Where will you need to spend some time helping people unlearn something that they think is true? Dislodging inaccurate information is a big challenge because people tend to discount information that doesn't confirm their prior beliefs. You'll need to be extra certain to have convincing data on hand for any points in this category. The good news is that if you can create what psychologists call a *curiosity gap* by surprising your audience with a fact they didn't know but that is credible, you might pique their attention. Rebecca was certainly surprised to see that the chronic absenteeism rate for kindergarten was about as high as the rates in high school, and she bets that other educators will be as well.

- *What new information do they need?* What information uncovered through your review of the research literature and your own data analysis must your audience know to get on board? Rebecca has found that her district's absenteeism rate is climbing and is higher than other similar districts' rates and that the same findings hold for each grade span. The data reveal a problem that deserves the district's attention. In addition, her analysis of the Hillside greetings strategy suggests it has helped slow down the rate of increase. This finding should be compelling for the district's elementary school teachers. And when she checked the randomized controlled trial described in "Attendance Playbook," she was persuaded that the Positive Greetings at the Door strategy (which included student greetings plus additional classroom-management tactics) had definitively caused better behavior and student engagement in a middle school context. She'll be sure to explain that finding to her skeptical middle school team.

- *What claims might they be suspicious of or disagree with?* Thinking through the answers to this question is another way to guard against your audience's cognitive biases. You know that people will be more likely to dismiss anything they disagree with, so you can be prepared with more detail to support your claims. Rebecca knows the middle school teachers are likely to be particularly suspicious about whether they could implement the strategy with adolescents. She will therefore be sure to describe the implementation findings from the experimental study. Most but not all teachers in the study used precorrections (reminding students what successful behavior is before they have an opportunity to behave otherwise during a task) daily, but all the teachers reported success at standing near the door and positively greeting their students daily—the part of the strategy Rebecca is asking her own staff to implement.

- *What questions will they have?* Try taking the viewpoint of your audience members to understand what they'll want to know. Often their viewpoint boils down to some version of "How does this affect me?" Rebecca knows that her team will want to hear the details of what they're being asked to do. Beyond that, she hopes that the task force members will want to examine how their own greetings strategy works out, since they are now more accustomed to asking "How do I know?"

Answering these questions for your own circumstances will help you prioritize which pieces of information you want to highlight, both from other people's research and from your own analyses. Your next task is to make this information accessible for your audience. This means invoking the power of examples, words, and visuals to tell your story.

Use a Concrete Example

Once you know which findings are most important, grab your audience's attention with a good example that can stand for the whole. Part of what makes the Edutopia videos so powerful is that, rather than reciting dry statistics or talking in generalities, it shows real-life examples of teachers and students to demonstrate the impact of personal relationships. Rebecca uses this same idea but adds her own spin. She sends two members of the absenteeism task force to see the greetings process at Hillside firsthand. They take a video of it in action and record interviews with a student and a teacher about the positive impact the greetings strategy has had on school culture. The crucial thing from an evidence perspective is that Rebecca selects an example that she has verified from her research. If Hillside had not seen positive initial results from the greetings strategy, it would be disingenuous to share a video or story suggesting that the strategy was having a positive impact.

Another version of this idea is to use specific data points, rather than summary statistics, when talking about quantitative data. While Rebecca could say, "In a typical kindergarten classroom in our district, four out of twenty-one students are likely to be chronically absent this year," this statement becomes even more powerful when changed to "In Irene Andrews's kindergarten classroom, four of her twenty-one students are likely to be chronically absent this year." (That is, of course, assuming Irene's classroom isn't unusual in some way that would make that statement inaccurate.) Once you have made these initial choices, you can move on to creating a narrative that will link your findings with words and visuals.

INTERPRET EVIDENCE WITH WORDS

The heart of sharing evidence with words is good writing. We will leave the general writing tips to the experts; see the Further Readings section for some suggestions. Instead we will focus on how you can use words to share what your audience needs to know about the evidence you've distilled.

Draft Your Findings

In chapter 5, we talked about how to use different kinds of comparisons to drive your data analysis. The first step in using those comparisons to interpret evidence with words is to draft a finding. A finding is a short statement or claim about what you have learned from a piece of analysis. When it's based on quantitative data, it should be a single sentence with a number in it. The statement can include more than one number to provide a comparison point—but beware that too many numbers can be hard to parse.

Writing findings is a great way to be sure you completely understand each number you see in a table or represented in a figure. Putting numbers into sentences will help you notice which ones are worth focusing on as you consider your next steps.

Here are some of the draft findings Erin shared with Rebecca:

- Last year, 21.8 percent of students in Lincoln School District were chronically absent.

- The district's overall chronic absenteeism rate is 21.8 percent, compared with 13.2 percent statewide and 19.2 percent in similar districts.

- The chronic absenteeism rate in Lincoln has increased by nearly 30 percent in the past five years.

- More than one in six kindergartners in Lincoln were chronically absent last year.

- Hillside had the highest absenteeism rate among elementary schools, at 17.8 percent.

- The chronic absenteeism rate at the middle school is 18.0 percent, compared with 10.8 percent at similar middle schools statewide.

These are all simple and straightforward statements based on data. The first finding does not include a comparison, as it is a basic fact about the issue of chronic absenteeism in the Lincoln School District. But as you may have noticed, it is not particularly useful on its own, because it provides no context for whether 21.8 percent is large or small. By adding comparisons through the next few bullets, Rebecca has made the importance of the issue more obvious. The comparison need not be explicit. For example, the third finding doesn't include the actual absenteeism rate from five years ago; it just states that the current rate is higher. However, as we'll discuss later in this chapter, the more concrete and specific the comparison, the better.

Rebecca could also draft findings to interpret results from others' existing research. She knows from her audience analysis that she will need to convince her middle school teachers of the value of this intervention for their grade span. After reviewing the results from the article about the randomized controlled trial of the Positive Greetings at the Door strategy, which took place in two middle schools, she drafts the following finding: "In middle school classes with past behavioral problems, classroom greetings combined with proactive classroom-management strategies increase students' time engaged on academics by one hour per day."

In this case, the researchers measured the impact of the initiative in hours per day. But academic studies often report impacts in terms of effect sizes, a statistical measure. Effect sizes require additional information to interpret and apply to practice; see the sidebar "Interpreting Effect Sizes" for further details.

Interpreting Effect Sizes

When you are reporting findings from your own data, you will usually use straightforward percentages, average scaled scores, and so forth. But if you have chosen to pull in some data from other research, particularly from causal analyses, you may find that the researchers have reported their findings in units of effect sizes. What the heck is an effect size?

In the context of causal inference, an effect size (sometimes called Cohen's *d* statistic) is the difference in average outcomes between those who received an intervention and those who did not, divided by the standard deviation (a measure of the spread, or variation, in the data). As we discussed earlier, despite its name, this statistic is only a measure of the effect of an intervention if the study is properly designed to demonstrate cause and effect. We would prefer the term *association size*, but we use *effect size* here since it is more commonly used in research.

Effect sizes fall between 0 and 1, with numbers closer to 1 indicating larger magnitudes; their magnitude does not depend on the unit of measure. Because they are all on the same scale, you can directly compare the magnitude of an intervention's association with, say, SAT scores and the intervention's association with grade 10 mathematics test scores. But effect sizes are much harder to interpret in practical terms than percentages or even scaled scores; to be meaningful to educators, they require further translation.

Researchers will often provide comparisons to help others interpret the effect sizes. For example, they may describe an effect size as "equivalent to a quarter of an average year's gain in reading achievement" or as something that "would close 10 percent of the typical black/white test score gap." If not, they may rely on effect-size benchmarks to help gauge magnitude. When Jacob Cohen originally invented this statistic, he suggested benchmarks of 0.2 for a small effect, 0.5 for moderate, and 0.8 for large.[1] Similarly,

John Hattie's *Visible Learning* promotes 0.4 as a benchmark for noticeable differences in outcomes. But recent research has shown that these benchmarks are too high and insufficiently nuanced for education interventions, especially for noncausal studies.

Instead, we recommend Matt Kraft's many helpful suggestions for interpreting effect sizes in education contexts.[2] Kraft argues for benchmarks of less than 0.05 for small, 0.05 to less than 0.2 for medium, and 0.2 or greater for large effect sizes in education (and he does mean effect, not association, size). He also makes the case that effect size on its own isn't enough information to make good decisions about which strategies to pursue, because interventions that generate a small impact but are low-cost and easy to scale might be more valuable than those that generate large impacts but impose high costs or a high degree of difficulty. Ultimately, it's up to you as an education leader to gauge how much all these factors matter in your situation and to use your common sense.

Rebecca recognizes that her middle school teachers might ask about the context for the study and how similar it is to Lincoln, so she makes few notes for herself: "Pacific Northwest; 68 percent nonwhite in one school, 73 percent in the other. FRPL 52 percent and 64 percent (similar to us). Six language arts classes, four math classes, 203 students. Two hours of teacher training plus follow-up feedback." She'll keep those notes in her back pocket just in case. She anticipates more questions about the strategy itself, as it is much more involved than what happened at Hillside and requires training, daily logs for teachers, and coaching for teachers with low implementation fidelity early on. These findings aren't final yet, but they serve as a good starting place for Rebecca to summarize and organize what she has learned so far.

Use Comparisons to Interpret What You Learn

When Rebecca asks herself, "What do my audience members think they know but really don't?" she realizes that her audience might not know that chronic absenteeism rates are very high in early grades. How can she convey this point in a way that will resonate powerfully with her audience?

Chip Heath and Dan Heath, brothers and authors of *Made to Stick: Why Some Ideas Survive and Others Die*, explain the importance of context in interpreting data: "Statistics aren't inherently helpful; it's the scale and context that makes them so."[3] Chapter 5 explained how you can use comparisons to make more convincing inferences from your data. Here, we'll argue that comparisons are also useful for establishing scale and context. How meaningful are the differences you found? How relevant? Whether your evidence comes from other people's research or data you analyzed yourself, getting the comparisons right will help others understand and relate to your findings, making them more powerful. The Heath brothers call this "making your data human scale."

Rebecca can use the types of comparisons we discussed in chapter 5 and the audience analysis questions from earlier in this chapter to amplify her findings. For example, rather than just saying that chronic absenteeism rates are high in early grades, she could phrase her finding this way: "Chronic absenteeism rates for our kindergartners are almost as high as they are for our ninth graders." This provides a comparison to what is likely to be a familiar reference point—absenteeism rates in high school—and creates a curiosity gap because of the unexpected finding. Table 6.1 shows more examples of how different types of comparisons can amplify quantitative findings and make them more powerful.

TABLE 6.1

Use comparisons to build more powerful findings	
TYPE OF COMPARISON	**REBECCA'S FINDINGS**
Compare findings to a goal	• Our chronic absenteeism rate is 21.8 percent, which is higher than the state average of 12.9 percent.
Compare findings over time	• Our chronic absenteeism rates have increased by more than 26 percent over the last five years.
	• In our district, 764 students missed 18 or more days of school last year, 132 more than five years ago.
Compare one element to other similar elements	• Our district's chronic absenteeism rate is 21.8 percent, a rate higher than anyone else's in our region.
	• More than a quarter of our kindergarteners are chronically absent, similar to the rate at the high school.
	• In a typical kindergarten classroom in our district, 4 out of 21 students are likely to miss 18 or more days of school this year.
Combine comparisons	• The increase in chronic absenteeism is growing 8 percent faster each year in kindergarten than it is at the high school.
Use lots of data to see patterns	• The number of days of school that students missed last year is strongly associated with how many they will miss this year.
Look to outliers to learn from extreme comparisons	• In our district, 54 students missed 20 percent or more of school days last year, and 26 missed 30 percent or more.
	• In Lincoln School District, 54 students missed 36 or more school days last year, and 26 missed 54 or more.

Rebecca uses the same principles of comparison in her draft finding from the Positive Greetings at the Door research project. That study combines two comparisons:

- *Compare one observation to similar others:* Middle school students in disruptive classrooms who were randomly assigned to doorway greetings and other behavioral interventions, versus others from similar classrooms who did not receive interventions.

- *Compare data over time:* Student academic engaged time before versus after the behavioral interventions.

Notice that as the comparisons become more specific, the evidence feels more human scale and memorable. Notice also that numbers tend to feel more tangible than do percentages or rates, whether the number of students who are chronically absent (763 versus 21.8 percent) or the amount of academic engaged time (one hour per five-hour school day versus 20 percent of a school day).

Use Technical Words Carefully

As you are doing your final editing, be careful with any language about cause and effect and about statistical significance. Only use cause-related words such as *affected, led to, followed from, resulted from, translated to,* and . . . well, *caused* when your data come from a well-designed study that allows you to infer causation. Otherwise, use words like *correlated, related to, linked to,* or *associated with* to describe relationships between variables. See the sidebar "Words to Watch Out for on Claims of Cause and Effect" in chapter 3 for more details. Yes, other people use all these words interchangeably. But you can take the high road by using the more accurate, less ambiguous terminology.

Be careful with the word *significant,* also. In common usage, *significant* means something large or meaningful (e.g., "My mother was a significant influence on my development"). Meanwhile, researchers sometimes sloppily use *significant* to describe any difference that is statistically different from zero, whether the difference is large or not. When reading others' work, be sure you understand how they are using this term. Be clear in your own communication, too. To avoid confusion, use the phrase *statistically significant* (rather than just *significant*) when describing the results of a statistical test. Describe the practical importance or magnitude of your findings with words like *substantial, large,* or *big* rather than *significant.* Take the high road here, too.

INTERPRET EVIDENCE THROUGH DATA DISPLAYS

When evidence comes in a quantitative form, you often need to show it in a chart, graph, or table to help your audience interpret it. Simple choices about how you design that data display can go a long way toward making your message resonate. Like interpreting evidence through words, interpreting evidence through a data display mainly comes down to using comparisons strategically to illustrate your point. We focus here on a few key points about data displays that make a big difference. For more resources on data visualization, see the Further Readings section.

Choose a Simple Display

When you are presenting data visually, the most crucial decision is what type of display to use. We strongly recommend that you stick with one of four simple data displays: bar charts, line graphs, scatterplots, and tables. They are familiar to many audiences, straightforward to interpret, and easy to format in a way that highlights the most important information. Each format is best for displaying different kinds of relationships within your data, as we show in figure 6.1, which we adapted from Stephen Few's *Show Me the Numbers*.[4] Rather than discuss each type of display individually here, out of context from Rebecca's findings and narrative, we will use examples of each type throughout this section.

You may have noticed that pie charts aren't on our recommended list. Despite their popularity, they are often tough to interpret. The way our brains perceive area makes it hard to accurately compare the sizes of two-dimensional areas formed from angles.[5] Small differences across groups will become almost imperceptible in a pie chart, even when they are still obvious in other formats.

To demonstrate the point, let's suppose you wanted to know more about which types of disabilities are most common among your chronically absent students with disabilities. In this situation, many educators would use a pie chart because the values they're examining are percentages that add up to 100. But compare the pie chart with the bar chart in figure 6.2. On the pie chart, it's hard to distinguish the share of students with disabilities from those with a speech impairment—and the differences between the three other categories are even harder to parse. But the bar chart makes all the differences in magnitude obvious.

For more on the problems with pie charts, we recommend Stephen Few's essay "Save the Pies for Dessert."[6] And if someone forces you into using one, check the data visualization part of our Further Readings section for suggestions on how to format them most effectively.

FIGURE 6.1

Data display options	
DISPLAY TYPE	**WHAT DOES THIS DISPLAY SHOW BEST?**
Bar chart 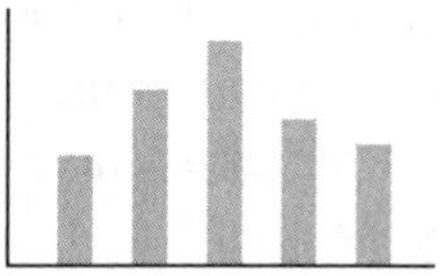	• Rankings, with data ordered from low to high or high to low • Differences in quantity or magnitude across groups • Part-to-whole relationships
Line graph 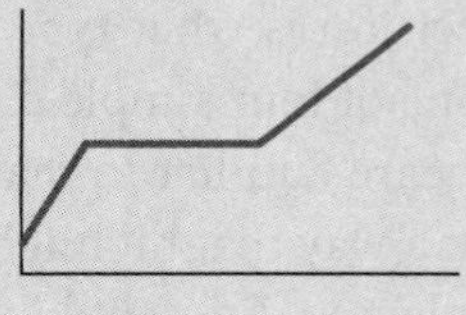	• Trends over time • Differences between groups in trends over time
Scatterplot 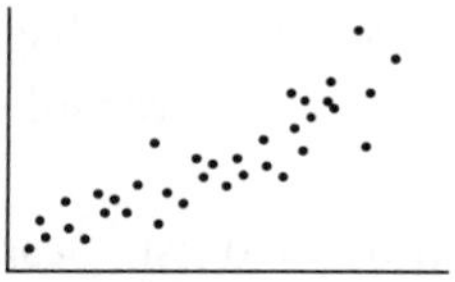	• Relationship between two variables when both variables take on many values
Table	• All the individual values for a variable or set of variables

Table shown under "Table":

Hillside	Lemont
55	32
59	25
84	20

A corollary: we recommend against using any graph types we haven't mentioned. Yes, you *can* make a radar graph, or a stacked area chart, or a doughnut chart, or a funnel chart. But they tend to look cluttered and will distract your audience from absorbing your message. The same goes for three-dimensional data displays. We have yet to see a circumstance where a three-dimensional format adds any real information to a graph. But we have seen many where it makes a graph harder to interpret.

FIGURE 6.2

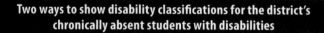

Two ways to show disability classifications for the district's
chronically absent students with disabilities

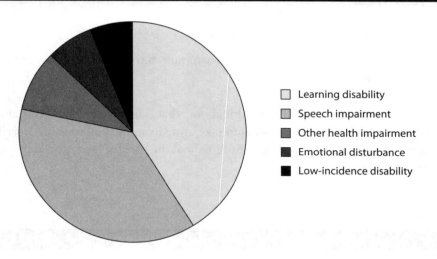

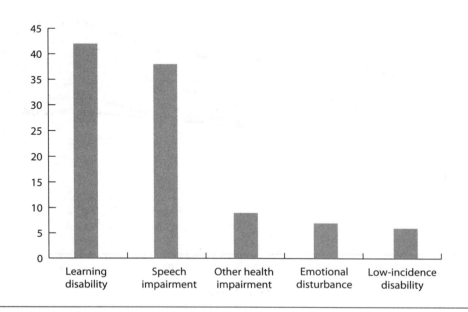

Turn Your Findings into Titles

Take a look at the line graph in figure 6.3. Now compare these two alternative titles for the graph:

- ▪ Chronic absenteeism rates over time

- ▪ Elementary school chronic absenteeism rates have increased by 25 percent

The first provides a topic but no hint about what is important about this analysis. The second shows the reader what to take away from the graphic and describes the magnitude of the most important finding, making the display much more powerful and persuasive.

FIGURE 6.3

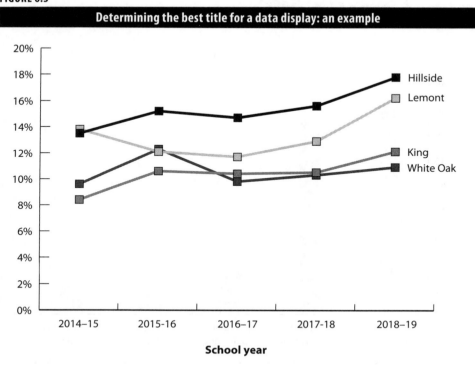

Determining the best title for a data display: an example

The most effective titles are more like headlines than like labels. They briefly and accurately describe the main takeaway using meaningful numbers, active verbs, and powerful words. They should stand on their own to tell readers the pattern you want them to focus on and how they should interpret it. Does this all sound familiar? That's because it's also how we defined a finding. Turning your findings into titles will make obvious which details your audience should notice first and how they should interpret the display.

Use Formatting to Draw Attention

Our brains perceive darker, thicker, and larger visual objects as more important; lighter, thinner, and smaller objects as less important. Use this human tendency to your advantage by varying the visual elements of your data display to highlight its most important elements.

For example, Rebecca wants to emphasize that the chronic absenteeism rates in kindergarten are much higher than her audience thinks they are. Figure 6.4A is her first draft of a bar chart showing grade-by-grade chronic absenteeism rates.

This draft is not bad. The audience members could easily compare the rates across the grade levels and see for themselves how the kindergarten is doing and how its rate that compares with that of ninth graders. But the chart could be better. One simple tweak, shown in figure 6.4B—making the kindergarten and ninth-grade bars darker than the others—immediately draws the eye to those grade levels, focusing the audience on the issue Rebecca is concerned with.

Another way to use formatting is to include visual benchmarks. In the state where Lincoln School District is located, chronic absenteeism was defined as being absent 10 percent of school days or more. This definition is a useful benchmark to include on a graph of absenteeism rates. See figure 6.5, where we have reformatted the scatterplot from figure 5.2, which plotted the percentage of students' days missed in 2017–2018 against the same variable in 2018–2019. The reformatted graph reduces visual clutter and removes all gridlines except for the lines at 10 percent of days missed in each year—the state's definition of chronic absenteeism. Removing the clutter allows the reader to quickly scan the graph for how many students are above and below that cutoff in each year, and how many exceeded it in both years.

More generally, the message of many graphs is one of comparison: Higher than what? Worse than what? Highlight those benchmarks or reference points for your audience to make obvious the most important comparisons.

FIGURE 6.4

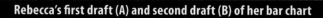

Rebecca's first draft (A) and second draft (B) of her bar chart

Chronic absenteeism is as high in kindergarten as it is in ninth grade

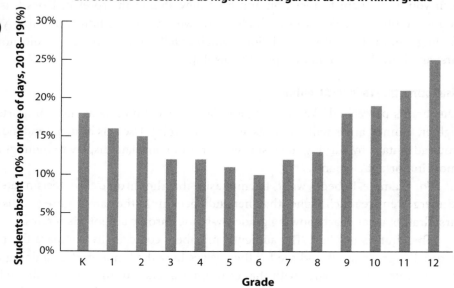

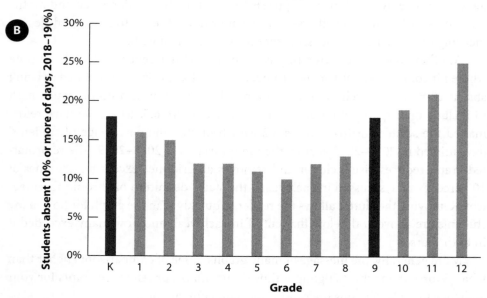

FIGURE 6.5

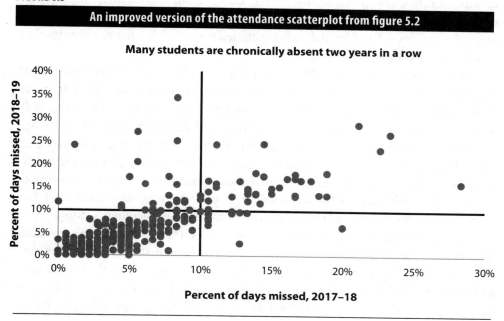

An improved version of the attendance scatterplot from figure 5.2

Many students are chronically absent two years in a row

Percent of days missed, 2018–19

Percent of days missed, 2017–18

Some final, small but important points for bar and line charts: bar charts should always be designed so the minimum vertical axis value is zero; beware that this is not always the default in graphing software. Starting from zero is less critical on line graphs, but the distance between the minimum and maximum values should take up about two-thirds of the chart area so that you don't over- or understate differences. Also, if you are using multiple line graphs with the same variable on the vertical axis, use the same minimum and maximum points for all of them. Using the same scale allows readers to make fair comparisons across graphs, since all vertical axes will be on the same scale, and it avoids magnifying any small differences.

Use Tables to Help Your Audience See Themselves in the Data

Tables are a great way to represent data when your audience wants to know or compare the values for a variable but the data are too numerous to be graphed easily—for example, the chronic absenteeism rate in every classroom in the district. Tables are also effective for comparisons across multiple units of measure. For example, you could show each classroom's average daily attendance and its chronic absenteeism rate side by side. And tabular displays can immediately increase relevance. A table with data for every school, for example, will allow every principal to see themselves in the data; if data are included for every classroom, every teacher will be able to do the same thing.

Because tables are dense with information, they often make better handouts or supplemental documents than they do content for summaries or slides. To make them more readable, you can remove the borders around each cell (many spreadsheets display borders by default) and place lines and shading strategically to reduce clutter, increase clarity, and focus the audience on the most important comparisons. It also helps to include the actual counts (e.g., number of students, number of teachers) in each cell, along with whichever percentage you think is likely to be the most relevant—the percentage of the row total, the column total, or the overall total. For more tips and examples, see "Data Displays" in the Further Readings section.

Rebecca asks Erin to make a table to hand out at the districtwide professional development day, showing the number and percentage of students in each classroom who have been chronically absent more than 10 percent of the school year so far (table 6.2). This visual will help emphasize that the absenteeism problem is pervasive in the district and that everyone needs to work together to resolve it.

TABLE 6.2

Attendance and absenteeism rates by classroom					
In nearly every classroom in the district, more than 10 percent of students have been chronically absent so far this year.					
			STUDENTS ABSENT 10% OF DAYS OR MORE		
DISTRICT, SCHOOL, OR CLASSROOM	GRADE	TOTAL ENROLLMENT	NUMBER	PERCENTAGE	AVERAGE DAILY ATTENDANCE
District	K–12	3,500	764	21.8	91.4
School:					
Hillside	*K–5*	*530*	*94*	*17.7*	*93.0*
Classroom:					
Diaz	K	21	3	14.3	93.4
Hart	K	22	5	22.7	95.7
Jones	K	19	2	10.5	92.5
Li	K	21	4	19.0	94.6

Note: This is only a part of the full table. It continues for the remaining schools and classrooms districtwide.

When you break down data to a fine-grained level of detail, you are likely to find situations where the story for one case is different from the average—for instance, a classroom where many fewer students are chronically absent than typical. These outliers are to be expected. Many values go into calculating an average; some may look much better (or worse) than the typical value, go into calculating an average. Situations like this can sometimes create uncomfortable conversations, though, particularly if your audience perceives the comparisons as unfair. For example, classrooms with the very highest absenteeism rates might also enroll many students whose special needs mean they are being educated in substantially separate settings. Your audience might believe that these classrooms skew the results. To counteract this concern, you might want to include additional data in the table. In this example, including the share of students with special needs in each classroom will help people understand which observations are most comparable. You can also think of those atypical cases as outliers, as discussed in chapter 5, and use them as a potential source for gathering ideas about best practices or practices to avoid.

USE EVIDENCE TO TELL A DATA STORY

Rebecca has built a body of information about chronic absenteeism in Lincoln School District from existing research and Erin's analysis, along with her own evaluation of what information her audience needs. Now she can pull together a set of clear, accurate, evidence-based claims that establish why this issue is important to her district and why she is asking teachers to change their practice. She can use these claims to organize her discussion of the absenteeism task force's results on the district professional development day. She assembles her claims, edits them, and arranges them into a series of talking points for her presentation.

She starts with a concrete example that stands in for the story, making sure to scale her numbers so they are easy to relate to and creating a curiosity gap by highlighting the findings she found most surprising:

Last week, I visited Irene Andrews's kindergarten class. I was surprised to learn that 4 of her 21 students had been absent at least four days so far, just two months into the school year.

It turns out that this rate is pretty representative of Lincoln's kindergarten classes. Last year, 50 out of our 280 kindergartners were chronically absent, meaning they were absent on 10 percent or more days of the school year. That's almost 20 percent of our kindergartners—4 or 5 students in every kindergarten classroom.

And that also means that our kindergartners are missing as much school as our ninth graders are missing.

Next, she provides more context on those findings and why this issue is important, beginning with what people already know (their own average daily attendance rates) and using comparisons to similar districts in the region to establish the problem. She also translates the definition of chronic absenteeism—missing 10 percent of days of enrollment or more—to a more tangible number, two days of school missed each month:

> We've known for years that Lincoln's average daily attendance rates were a little below other districts in our region. A typical student in our district misses eight days of school each year; in the rest of the region, it's more like five or six days.
>
> But now that chronic absenteeism is included in our school ratings in the state's accountability system, we've discovered that we have a problem we hadn't noticed before. One out of every 6 students in our district is absent 10 percent or more of the school year. That's eighteen days or more each year—two each month. That's a lot of instructional time missed.
>
> That's why I put together an absenteeism task force this year, chaired by Erin Frazier from Lemont, to learn more about what's going on with attendance in Lincoln and what we can do to improve it. Their work will continue all year, but here's what we've learned so far. We found that across Lincoln, in every grade and in every school, our chronic absenteeism rates are higher than they are in the rest of the region.

Now she uses the power of disaggregated data, providing Erin's table with the chronic absenteeism rates for every classroom in the district to demonstrate that the issue is pervasive and relevant to everyone:

> Take a look at the handout I passed around, and you'll see that in just about every classroom in the district, large numbers of students are chronically absent. So this isn't a problem for just some of us. It's a problem for all of us.

She adds a comparison over time and broadens her focus beyond accountability to the educational impact of absenteeism:

> And it's getting worse. Five years ago, 586 students missed eighteen or more days of school. Last year, it was 763. That's a 30 percent increase in just five years. And our enrollment has stayed steady, so the increase in numbers isn't coming from enrollment growth.
>
> This is worrisome, not just because of the accountability system, but also because many students are missing lots of school. We want to make sure we do everything we can to get students to school every day.

Next, she shares some background on the classroom greeting intervention she wants to implement, including the results of her difference-in-differences analysis, and explains what she wants her team to do:

> But the task force also found a bright spot. It turns out that the Hillside School implemented a program last year that may help. The teachers there made a point of welcoming every student to class every day with a personal greeting: students who wanted a physical welcome could choose a fist bump, handshake, or hug. Teachers did it because they thought it might improve their school climate and help students feel welcome and included at school.
>
> When we looked at the data, we saw that the greetings seems to have slowed down the rate of increase in chronic absenteeism at Hillside. We looked at the change in chronic absenteeism at Hillside from 2017, before the staff started the greetings, to 2018, afterward. And we compared that change to what was happening at Lemont, which has similar students but which didn't do greetings, just in case something was happening districtwide that affected both these schools at the same time. We found that both schools' chronic absenteeism rates increased, but Hillside's increased more slowly. Hillside's absenteeism rate the second year was 13.8 percent higher than its earlier rate, but Lemont's was 25.6 percent higher.
>
> That's why the task force has already recommended that all our elementary and middle schools do something similar this year, even while they're still working out recommendations for the longer-term plan. I think the greetings strategy is a great idea. I'd like every classroom teacher in the elementary schools, and every homeroom teacher in the middle school, to do just what Hillside did last year: greet every student personally every day. We have time built in later in this meeting to show you a video from the Hillside team about how this worked. We also want to get ideas from you about exactly how to implement this in your buildings and what challenges you anticipate, so that we can address them early.
>
> We will need to do more than just classroom greetings to get our absenteeism rates where we all want them. But this initial effort will get us started quickly and cheaply while the task force works on developing a longer-term strategy.

Finally, Rebecca describes how she will evaluate the implementation of the strategy and its impact so that her staff knows what to expect. She realizes that she can't make within-district comparisons as she did before, since everyone will be implementing the program at the same time. She plans for a regional comparison instead:

> I also want to make sure we learn from one another as we develop and implement this plan. We are going to be collecting data that will let us see how things are going along the way so we can adjust midcourse, and we'll run an analysis similar to the comparison of Hillside and Lemont at the end of the year to see if it made

a difference. This time, since everyone will be implementing the strategy at once, we'll compare changes in chronic absenteeism rates in our schools to changes in the rest of the region, which the state posts on its website.

I'm confident we can make a difference on our absenteeism rates so that more of our kids are in school every day and can benefit from the great instruction you all offer.

She saves a few key points in case she gets questions. She's particularly concerned about the middle school teachers' reaction, so she pulls out the details of the Positive Greetings at the Door intervention, especially how the demographics of those schools compare with her own district schools—differences that she had noted when she read the study. Armed with this information, she is better prepared to respond if the middle school staff questions a claim.

As you know, no matter how compelling your data display or how concrete your examples, your evidence alone won't be enough to convince anyone to change. You will also need to employ the other skills you have in your toolbox as an education leader. Skills such as change management, strategic planning, implementation monitoring, collaboration, and negotiation will all come into play. And you'll need to enlist your team in the hard work of implementation and evaluation and gather feedback from them along the way. But starting from a strong evidence base as you solve your problems, sharing that evidence in a clear and compelling way, and planning to gather more evidence on your practice will help you and your district make better bets.

KEY TAKEAWAYS

* Interpreting your findings for your audience is a crucial step in your analysis because it helps your audience make sense of what you have learned.

* The evidence you highlight should be specific to your audience and its needs. Start with what they already know and build their knowledge from there, paying particular attention to bringing strong evidence on issues they might disagree with or question.

* Use a concrete example of your findings to bring your results to life.

* In describing your results or findings, use short sentences that include a claim and a number. Make statistics "human scale" through relevant, understandable comparisons.

* Start with a simple, uncluttered data display, and use formatting elements such as size, shading, and benchmarks to draw your audience's attention to the most important comparisons.

* Use tables to provide detailed breakouts that will let your audience members see themselves in your data and compare themselves with others.

APPLY YOUR LEARNING

☐ Use the list of five questions presented in "Five Questions for Selecting the Evidence Your Audience Needs" in this chapter to decide on the information your audience needs to know. These might come from existing research, your own analyses, or both.

☐ See if you can identify a good concrete example of your most important finding.

☐ Choose one (or more) of the findings on your prioritized list. What type of comparison is it? How can you reframe the comparison to put the numbers on a human scale? Have you unintentionally used inaccurate language around causality or statistical significance? Refine your finding as needed.

☐ For the same finding, what data display type would work best? How can you use formatting to draw attention to the most important comparisons in the display? Would it be helpful to create a handout with a table breaking those numbers down further? Create an appropriate data display for the finding, using your finding as a title. As you work, notice how your formatting choices change its impact.

7

BUILD AND SUSTAIN EVIDENCE USE IN YOUR ORGANIZATION

The school year has just ended, and Superintendent Rebecca Sisti and her leadership team are starting to plan their work for the next year in detail. "I'd like to thank Erin Frazier and the absenteeism task force for putting together some great recommendations for our district to improve our chronic absenteeism rates," says Rebecca. "I'm excited about trying the new initiatives our board agreed to for next year, like text messaging reminders and an expanded school breakfast program. And it looks like our absenteeism rates ticked down a bit in the elementary and middle schools. I'm looking forward to seeing the results from our impact evaluation of the greetings strategy program, once we can get the comparison data for attendance rates at other schools in the region."

Principal Dennis Bollinger chimes in. "I'm so glad we put in that extra effort when we started the task force last year to compare the changes in absenteeism rates for Hillside and Lemont over time. If we had only looked at Hillside's chronic absenteeism rate before and after we started the doorway greetings, we would have thought that the greetings didn't matter—or maybe even made things worse. But by comparing Hillside to Lemont, we could see that the greetings strategy might actually be helping, by slowing down the rate of increase."

"Yes, that was really powerful," Rebecca says. "It makes me wonder about where else we could be doing more careful analysis that would help us better understand what's working in our district."

"Well," says Joe Victor, the high school principal, "last year we asked our guidance counselors to track our college applicants' financial aid applications more closely, to make sure students didn't fall through the cracks. It looks like more students completed their applications on time. But maybe they would have done that anyhow. I wonder if we could get some better comparison data to see if we really did improve, or if any research might give us some insights about what else we could do to simplify the financial aid process."

Sara Kramer, the director of student services, listens to everyone's comments with interest. "We could also do a better job on understanding our issues in the first place," she says. "I've heard that research says that English learners take three to five years to become proficient in oral English, and even longer for academic proficiency. But I've never checked out the research behind that claim. And although I know those numbers are about right for many of our English learners, I haven't looked into which students take longer, or why."

"I agree," says Rebecca. "We sometimes miss those opportunities. We could definitely do more to use research as part of how we develop our plans and evaluate ourselves. So, how can we make research a bigger part of how we do our work?"

From reading this book, you already know what constitutes useful evidence. You also know why it's so important to include evidence in your decision-making and in answering questions about your own work. But what might not be so obvious is *when* and *how* to get more evidence into your local conversations—that is, how to create and sustain the organizational conditions that increase the use of evidence.

We have good news for you: you don't need to create a new committee or book any more meetings to use evidence better. You'll need to contemplate how to redesign your organization's routines to support greater evidence use, and you'll need to commit to sticking with the change—as you would for any other organizational change worth making. But even incremental changes will make a difference and will create momentum for more. How to lead organizational change is a topic for another book. What we offer in this book is suggestions for shifts in practices to increase your use of evidence. How you implement these changes is up to you; you can apply whichever change management process you prefer.

This chapter lays out suggestions for organizations at beginning, intermediate, and advanced levels of expertise in using research. The shifts that are appropriate for beginning levels of research require little in the way of resources and expertise. As cultural shifts, these suggestions are not necessarily easy to implement, but they are accessible to anyone committed to the work—and they will be important pieces of the infrastructure you'll need if you are to build and sustain a culture of evidence use for the long term. We also provide details on additional intermediate and advanced shifts your district might consider as it gains more experience and expertise in evidence use.

BEGINNER SHIFTS: SMALL CHANGES THAT ADD UP TO BIG DIFFERENCES

Increase Your Exposure to Research

You encounter research in small ways all the time: in traditional media, at conferences, in talking with colleagues, from email distribution lists and messaging platforms, on social media, and through podcasts. By shifting your sources of information, you can easily increase the amount of education research you are exposed to. This change will be particularly helpful for increasing your conceptual use of research, that is, using research to define problems, get new ideas, or create new frameworks.

Add to your routine a few sources known for reporting accurately on research findings, to increase the likelihood that the information you obtain is backed by strong evidence. These sources could be mass media, materials from your professional association, or even a journal or two. (Pro tip: Put print copies in the staff lounge when you're done with them, and forward emails from these sources to your colleagues. These steps will send a signal that reading research is a valuable way to spend work time.) When it comes time to make an important decision, you need to track down the information behind any influential claims before acting on them.

If you, like us, have too much to read already, take a careful look through your usual sources. Are there a few you could cut out or cut back on to make a little more space for useful research? In particular, consider cutting sources that you notice conflating correlation and causation, equating stories from single studies with findings from a body of research, or excluding important methodological details about the research they report on.

Build Evidence Use into Existing Routines

All districts have annual planning, budgeting, monitoring, hiring, performance evaluation, professional development, and grading cycles, along with more frequent project or leadership meetings, planning sessions, and briefings. Many districts even have routines tied to data use, such as data teams or performance management processes. Designed thoughtfully, these routines create regular occasions for people to ask questions about evidence, consider its implications, and develop plans for change.

Where a formal data routine exists, it will naturally open conversations about evidence because people will already be asking questions about what their data say about progress on local priorities. Then your task is to encourage careful thinking about how to design those inquiries to gather the strongest evidence possible. You might also seek out new research to help inform how your team responds to challenges they uncover in your data. In Rebecca's case, she had no existing district-level data routine to work from. But she still made progress by sharing local research through a different routine: the upcoming districtwide professional development day.

Another way to take advantage of existing routines is to set aside time on meeting agendas to discuss recent research pertinent to your current work. Use our guiding questions from chapter 3 to discuss as a team the relevance and quality of the findings for your needs. Consider prioritizing articles that summarize multiple sources of evidence or selecting several individual articles on the same topic, so that you emphasize looking at the full body of evidence rather than just some pieces.

However you use your routines, keep in mind that you can't just hand out articles and expect people to read and understand them. Instead, build in opportunities to discuss and interpret how the findings would apply in your own situation. Discussion like this allows team members to learn both from one another and from the material and to build their skills in understanding and applying evidence—crucial capabilities for increasing the likelihood that evidence actually informs practice.

Ask "How Do We Know?" to Build a Culture of Evidence Use

Creating and sustaining a culture of asking "How do we know?" might be the single most important thing you can do to promote greater evidence use—whether you're in a position to influence that norm organization-wide or you work only within a team or an office. The question will drive people to share more convincing and relevant evidence. It mitigates against confirmation bias by forcing people to slow down and think through the evidence base for the claims they make. And it promotes equity by pushing for deeper analysis on how we know whether all students have access to the same resources, opportunities, and strategies.

All organizations have norms—implicit or explicit—about how team members should interact. Many even have formal ground rules agreed to by all team members. Common ones include "be present," "balance your participation with others," "disagree without being disagreeable," and "assume good intent." But we have rarely seen education organizations explicitly state that using evidence or backing up claims with data is a valued norm. This absence is notable in part because it conveys the lower priority that evidence gets in education decision-making today but also because without such a norm, people may feel personally attacked if a colleague starts demanding to see the data behind an assertion.

Norms are only effective to the extent that they are actively enacted. One way to maintain norms is to agree with your team about how you will signal each other if a norm is broken, to hold yourselves accountable. Our colleagues at Data Wise have done role-playing along these lines, where groups agree to "raise an eyebrow, tap their chin, or even hum when they feel a norm is being broken."[1] Another option is to assign a rotating devil's advocate who will question the assumptions behind people's claims and demand better evidence. Making the skeptic an official role in a meeting depersonalizes the evidence conversation, as people can blame the role rather than the person if their questions make clear that the evidence was weaker than originally thought.

You should also check in periodically on implementation of the norms your team has already agreed to. The check-in could take the form of a group discussion or an anonymous survey. Where weaknesses are identified, the group can discuss how to fix them. For more on creating and upholding group norms, see Kathryn Parker Boudett and Meghan Lockwood's essay, "The Power of Team Norms."[2]

INTERMEDIATE SHIFTS: EMBED EVIDENCE USE IN POLICY AND PRACTICE

Conduct a More Convincing Pilot, or Use Existing Randomization to Evaluate a Program

Dennis's greetings strategy in the Hillside School was a pilot, though an unintentional one: he had heard about an appealing idea and decided to try it. Educators frequently pilot-test new ideas, programs, and strategies before implementing them broadly, to work out any kinks in implementation and see whether they appear to have the intended impact. But, like Dennis, too often they don't plan for a thorough evaluation of the impact. Dennis lucked out that another school in his district, Lemont, looked similar enough to Hillside that he could use it as a comparison. But sometimes, a reasonable comparison group is not available, and as you know by now, the strongest evaluation design would rely on some form of random assignment to treatment and comparison groups.

You can use the principles you have learned about determining the relevance and convincingness of evidence and using your own data to start to design a more convincing pilot. The approach is the same as that for designing any impact evaluation, just at a smaller scale. Most of the time, you will not be able to (or want to) run a randomized controlled trial. But now that you know how valuable random assignment is to demonstrating that a strategy caused an outcome, you might see some opportunities to introduce randomization as you implement programs. Let's consider a few examples.

If you are implementing a program that has more applicants or eligible participants than you can serve, you could use a lottery to decide who participates. Lotteries are a form of random assignment, and they have the advantage of often being perceived as more equitable than giving access to an opportunity on a first-come-first-served basis or by application. Your evaluation then compares those who randomly won the lottery (and therefore got to participate) with those who randomly lost. If you take this approach, you must ensure that the lottery process is totally fair and transparent, so that people don't think some participants had a better chance than others did to win.

If you are implementing a program that you will be scaling up over several years, you could randomly assign students (or schools, or grades or classrooms within a school) to implement earlier versus later. In this scenario, you can't serve everyone at once anyhow; if you decide by random assignment when the students or other groups will start participating in the program, then you enjoy the benefit of randomization to help you evaluate the program's impact. In the first year of the program, your analysis would compare outcomes in that year for participants versus nonparticipants. In the following year, you could compare participants and nonparticipants again, and you could also make a three-way comparison: participants in their first year of implementation (irrespective of which year they started) versus participants in their second year versus nonparticipants.

If you select students to participate in a program on the basis of a test score or another cutoff for eligibility—say, a magnet program for gifted students—you could compare outcomes for students who are just above the cutoff score with those who are just below. This approach takes advantage of the arbitrary nature of all cutoffs. The students who are just above the cutoff are similar to those just below; the only difference is that the ones above the cut were eligible to participate in the program, and the ones below weren't. Researchers call this method a *regression discontinuity design*, but you don't have to run a regression to use it. For a reasonable estimate, you can compare the outcomes for the students just above the cutoff and the outcomes for those just below. It's important to check that those below didn't end up participating, anyhow, for example, because their parents successfully lobbied to have them switched into the program. Also, this approach only tells you the impact of the program *for those near the cutoff point*, not for everyone.

Even if you lack an opportunity to randomize who is treated in your pilot, you can still benefit from a more convincing research design by collecting baseline outcomes data for both participants and nonparticipants. That way, you won't be stuck after the fact trying to find some sort of comparative data for evaluating your program. You should also plan to collect data on how closely the program implementation tracks to what you ideally had in mind, so that you can troubleshoot if things start to go awry.

When piloting programs, you'll find it worthwhile to take a little time up front to document the analyses you want to conduct later. Even if you're clear now on how you'll handle your data, in our experience, those details fade fast. Take a few moments to jot down your ideas in a way that will make sense when you come to it cold. Now is also a good time to schedule when you will analyze the data for the evaluation. You know when the data you need should be available; block out some time on your calendar shortly thereafter, and note where you saved your evaluation plan (not that either of us has ever forgotten where we filed a document!). Planning your analysis is also useful to reduce the impact of cognitive biases that make you think you "just know" how well the strategy worked.

Commit in Advance to the Criteria for Action

Another way to mitigate against seeing what you want to see in your data is to decide in advance, before you see the outcome data, which criteria you will use for deciding on an action. That is, you can ask yourself, "How do I know that the difference is convincing enough for me to act?"—and, crucially, not change your mind after you see the results. That way, your decision can't be influenced by the results.

Maria Gonzalez and her team of math teachers could use this advance-commitment strategy to decide whether to continue the reteaching program. Before they begin the intervention, they could decide how big an improvement on the state test they would need to see, and at what cost, to justify sticking with that strategy. For example, they could say that the eighth graders would need to at least improve at the same rate as seventh graders did in the first year to make reteaching worth continuing. The teachers might look for an even faster rate of improvement in the second year, figuring that they would still be working out the kinks in the first year. Or they might decide that they would continue the strategy only if they saw a positive impact and if reteaching took no more than one day out of each curriculum unit. If both these criteria could not be met—for example, if the program was too time-intensive—the teachers would consider a tiered or triaged intervention instead.

This judgment may be subjective, particularly where cost-benefit analyses are not readily available, and that's fine. The point is to force yourself to think through all the issues and tradeoffs in the decision *before* you see your outcome data through the rose-colored glasses you inevitably put on after you have invested your time and effort into implementing a new program.

It takes discipline to stick with your predetermined decisions, especially when the evidence leans against your preferred outcome. You may be tempted to say, "Yeah, but . . ." and generate a host of reasons why your program didn't have the impact you had expected. It might help to commit publicly to your decision—for example, by saying to your superintendent or school board that you will only continue or expand a program if you can demonstrate an impact of a certain magnitude or greater.

Create a Learning Agenda

So far in this book, we have shown how to build a set of analyses that advance and improve a single strategy. In our experience, as educators become familiar with how to build and use evidence to improve their work, they tend to find many opportunities to use these tools. After you have logged some successes, you may want to create a *learning agenda*: a document that describes the questions an organization is trying to answer about its work (that is, what it wants to learn) and how and when it will answer them. A learning agenda anticipates the questions your district will have months or years down the line, so that you can plan for the data and resources you'll need to answer them. It helps mitigate against crisis management by making you think forward, not backward.

For example, Erin has drafted a learning agenda for the Lincoln School District's chronic absenteeism work (table 7.1). The first two items relate to the greetings strategy they are trying out. Many of the others came from the sticky notes the team members generated when they brainstormed about the causes of chronic absenteeism and from their initial reading of "Attendance Playbook." Notice that they have triaged their analysis to focus first on evaluating the doorway greetings strategy, then better understanding the causes of chronic absenteeism in their district, and finally evaluating strategies that might help the district reduce its absenteeism rates overall or for certain types of students.

TABLE 7.1

Lincoln School District's learning agenda on chronic absenteeism			
QUESTION	HOW WILL WE ANSWER THE QUESTION?	PRIORITY	WHEN NEEDED
Are elementary and middle teachers implementing the doorway greetings strategy?	Collect data through hallway checks	High	End of February
Does implementing doorway greetings improve attendance? Reduce chronic absenteeism?	Compare trends in absenteeism rates	High	Initial analysis end of February; final end of school year
Is chronic absenteeism a bigger problem for students with disabilities? Students who move homes or schools? Students experiencing homelessness or in foster care? Other student groups?	Analyze internal data	Medium	By April
Can we predict which students are likely to be chronically absent each year, so that we can intervene earlier?	Analyze internal data	Medium	By April
Is absenteeism higher in schools that have more problems with bullying?	Collect new school climate data about bullying, then analyze	Medium	By April
Is our student discipline system contributing to chronic absenteeism?	Analyze internal data	Low	By next school year
What strategies might help reduce chronic absenteeism in Lincoln School District, either overall or for particular groups of students?	Review existing research	High	End of school year
How many of our chronically absent students could benefit from the strategies identified in existing research (e.g., access to breakfast, laundry at school, community mentors)?	Analyze internal data	Medium	By April

Taking the time to build a learning agenda helps you organize and prioritize the research under way and identify gaps where no research is planned but is needed. And over time, implementing the agenda items will help you build a body of evidence about your work. One person can develop a learning agenda individually. But the agenda becomes an even more powerful tool when a leadership team and program staff work together to develop one. Doing so will identify areas about which the team members have different assumptions or aspirations, as well as areas where more evidence is needed to inform a decision.

To put this agenda into motion, Erin will need to figure out additional details, such as who is responsible for each of these projects, what data they will need, and what comparisons they will make. Those details can be tracked in the learning agenda itself or developed into separate project plans or study designs. Down the line, if Lincoln builds a learning agenda for all district priorities, not just absenteeism, the district might find that it also needs a summary document listing the high-level questions for each area, to help keep the big picture in view.

How will you know that you are ready to create a learning agenda? If you have reached the following milestones, you are probably ready:

- You have already successfully completed several inquiries using the tools in this book, ideally touching more than one program or office in your district.

- You have, in at least several parts of the district, leaders who see evidence as part of their strategy for improvement, not as a task on top of their work, and these leaders are willing to ask questions and update their beliefs as they acquire more information.

- You have someone on staff who is willing to lead the learning agenda's development, implementation, and monitoring as part of their work.

- Ideally, you have an districtwide strategic plan that identifies your highest-priority initiatives.

Generate Questions for a Learning Agenda

The key to developing a useful learning agenda is asking the right questions of yourself and your team. It may seem like the obvious place to start is, "Are our current strategies working?" But as you know from reading this book, your existing strategies were probably not designed to answer that question well. You might not have the baseline data you need to make appropriate comparisons, or you might not have any data at all.

How do you avoid this problem? Instead of looking backward, look forward. Think about what challenges or other issues you expect to confront in the next few years. Carrie and two colleagues from another state education agency recently wrote an essay that suggested considering these questions:

- What are your priorities?

- What problems are you trying to solve?

- What decisions or changes are on the horizon?

- What are you uncertain about or wish you knew more about in those areas?

- What makes the work challenging?[3]

These types of questions will generate ideas rather than discourage them and will work better with the slower timelines that research often requires. As you start to fill in the list of the upcoming issues for which research might help, use diagnosis, implementation, and impact questions to refine and deepen your agenda. Pushing to this next level of questioning will help ensure that you carefully think through the question "How do I know?" (or "How would I know?") before you act. Asking this question may also reveal gaps in your agenda—where you have questions but no plan to answer them—and can help you reset priorities.

Winnow Down Your Questions

As your team gets used to this type of approach, you may find that the members generate far more questions than what you can answer with the available resources. If that's the case, have the team prioritize the questions using a question prioritization matrix—a two-by-two grid with difficulty of execution marked on the horizontal axis and impact on the vertical (figure 7.1). (This is a great tool for prioritizing any large number of tasks.)

Draw the two axes on a whiteboard, or put up some chart paper, and label them like the axes in figure 7.1. Write each research question on a sticky note, and have the team decide together where they would place it along each of the two

FIGURE 7.1

Question prioritization matrix	
Definitely pursue	**Pursue judiciously; consider using external partners**
Pursue a few for potential future needs	**Avoid**

High impact *(upper row)* · Low impact *(lower row)*
Easy to execute *(left column)* · Difficult to execute *(right column)*

dimensions. You don't need to quantify this, so don't overthink it. Just arrange the sticky notes in relative order using your best group judgment. Once you've completed that exercise for all your questions, you can use their placement to help prioritize. Questions that are high impact and easy to execute are low-hanging fruit. Questions that are high impact but difficult to execute are also worth pursuing, but do so judiciously. Select just a few to ensure you don't overtax your resources, and consider how external partners might help (see the next section, "Work with an External Researcher"). Questions that are low impact and difficult to execute should probably come off the list.

In the final category—low impact and easy to execute—Carrie has been surprised at the number of times that these questions have turned out to be worth investigating over the long run, as priorities change. For example, what started as a graduate student's nice-to-have analysis of the impact of attending Massachusetts technical high schools evolved, years later, into a stream of projects about career and technical education statewide, once a new governor was elected and made that program a top priority. So even though the questions seem low impact now, you might select a few of these to pursue. They can make good assignments for interns or junior staff seeking additional responsibilities or for untested external researchers seeking to work with you, because the questions are helpful but not immediately consequential if the project doesn't work out.

Work with an External Researcher

Now that you have a better understanding of the value of evidence and maybe even a more convincing pilot or a learning agenda under your belt, you may have pressing questions that would be too much work for your own team to handle or that would require skills your team doesn't have. One way to enlist additional resources is to work with external researchers such as university faculty members or research consulting firms.

Most researchers studying education issues care deeply about having an impact on practice, so they are eager to do work in practice settings. They are always looking for access to new data and settings to conduct studies, and they often need real-world class projects for their students. External researchers also bring an independent, external view to your programs, which is especially important when a question is politically sensitive and you don't want to be perceived as having your thumb on the scale for a particular result. Also, because many researchers are experienced at writing grants to support their work, you may not need to pay them directly for their services.

Unfortunately, these relationships all too often leave the district partner dissatisfied, because not all researchers are equally skilled at working with practitioners. Some outside researchers seem interested only in taking your data and producing academic papers of limited value to you; others may not respond to your priorities and timelines. Even the best relationships will require an investment of your time to ensure that these external partners have enough information and access to your internal experts to answer the right questions for your needs.[4]

Identify the Best Projects for External Researchers

How do you know which types of projects are best done internally and which lend themselves to external assistance? Internal analysis may be best if you already have the data you need to answer the question, the project needs a quick turnaround, or you want to maintain control over messaging and publication. Internal projects are often more oriented toward planning and the prioritization of resources and are typically less sophisticated analytically. External researchers may be helpful where a project requires new data collection or sophisticated analytical methods, or where a third-party analysis is important for the credibility of the findings. Outside parties may also have access to grant resources to support their research—and sometimes even to support the program itself, especially in earlier phases of development.

As noted above, the best types of projects for a first foray with a new researcher, in our experience, are from the low-impact, easy-to-execute quadrant in the question prioritization matrix. It takes time to build up the relationships and institutional knowledge to pull off a strong project with a new researcher, so choosing a time-sensitive topic will inevitably lead to frustration. Getting more information on a nice-to-have will hopefully set you up to solve a future challenge you anticipate, but it also won't be a crisis if the project goes poorly.

The best researchers to work with can demonstrate that they have expertise in the field you're interested in *and* that they know how to work effectively with organizations like yours. Look for people with prior experience doing research on related topics with districts, states, or education nonprofits, and ask questions about the nature of their relationship with their partner. Did they just get data from the agency and come back six months later with an answer, or did they collaborate more closely? If so, how did they structure those interactions? Did the first project lead to more collaboration, or was it a one and done? Are the written products from their previous projects similar to what you would want for your own project in terms of readability and tone? Contact others who have previously worked with the research team to ask about their experiences as well.

Ensure the Appropriate Level of Confidentiality, and Conduct the Research Ethically

A crucial decision you'll need to make is the level of confidentiality you will want the researchers to maintain about your district and your students. At the district level, does the sensitivity of the findings mean you want your district to remain anonymous in any later publications? Or is it okay if you are named, potentially helping others establish relevance?

At the student level, most research projects require access to confidential student data to produce useful analysis. The Family Education Rights and Privacy Act (FERPA) allows you to release personally identifiable information about students for research purposes under certain conditions, including executing a signed written agreement on the specific requirements for how the researchers will maintain the confidentiality of the data (see the sidebar "Personally Identifiable Information Under FERPA"). The federal Privacy Technical Assistance Center has created a helpful checklist for what these written agreements must contain.[5] You should

Personally Identifiable Information Under FERPA

Access to personally identifiable information about students is governed federally by the Family Education Rights and Privacy Act (FERPA). Under FERPA, personally identifiable information includes direct identifiers such as student name, address, and social security and local identification numbers, as well as indirect identifiers such as date and place of birth and "other information that, alone or in combination, is linked or linkable to a specific student that would allow a reasonable person in the school community, who does not have personal knowledge of the relevant circumstances, to identify the student with reasonable certainty."[6]

Simply removing the name and date of birth is usually not enough to make student-level data not personally identifiable, because of the provision around the combination of data elements that together could identify a child. As soon as even one child can be individually identified through a combination of data elements in a data set—for example, the one Black student in the fifth grade in a school that is almost entirely White—the whole data set is considered personally identifiable. These data can still be disclosed for research purposes, but the disclosure must meet the additional requirements set forth in the FERPA regulations.

take advantage of this provision to disclose the data necessary for researchers to conduct their work, but you also should hold them to high expectations about how the data will be held and what will happen to it after the project ends. This territory gets complicated quickly, and state and local laws may also apply, so consult your legal counsel for advice.

Set Clear Expectations and Deliverables

Once you've found a potential external researcher to work with, you'll need to create routines for reviewing study designs, early findings, and so forth, to get what you want out of the work. Remember, the researchers are not doing you a favor. You have the data and access they want, and you may even be paying them for the work. Use that leverage to make sure you get what you need from the project.

Researchers often want to keep finessing their analyses until their findings are final before showing them to you, just in case their results change. But you will want to have a sense of the likely findings earlier on so that you can start to plan your response. You will also want a chance to provide feedback in case they misunderstood something about your context or used your data incorrectly. Insist on intermediate deliverables. For example, ask for a systematic literature review (as a bonus, this request saves you from having to dig up and evaluate all the prior research yourself). You should also insist on an outline of the proposed report, the results from any preliminary descriptive analysis *before* the researchers start running fancy statistical models, a sneak peek at early findings, and briefings for you and your staff throughout the project. That way, you will have plenty of opportunities to learn from and redirect the work. You should also require an executive summary appropriate for public distribution and any other final deliverables you may want (perhaps a PowerPoint deck or infographic summarizing the findings) along with whatever technical report the group will produce.

Multiple deliverables paired with in-person meetings also help build strong connections between everyone involved in the project: the researchers, the district leadership, and the program staff. This approach substantially increases the chances that the findings from the work will matter for practice; as a bonus, it builds evidence literacy in your organization. Early in her time at the state agency, Carrie would often develop projects with external researchers on her own, rather than (in her perception) "bothering" the program staff with the details. This approach, it turns out, virtually guarantees that the research will not make an impact. If staff can't contribute to the research questions, provide feedback on early findings, and discuss the implications of those findings, they won't be invested in the project or as likely to use its results to change their practice.

Don't Ask a Question You Don't Want to Know the Answer To

One final, important note about working with outside researchers: don't ask them to answer a question you don't want to know the answer to. An important professional value held by researchers is academic freedom: "full freedom in research and in the publication of results," including their ability to freely express ideas and opinions without fear of retribution.[7] A researcher with integrity would never change or agree not to publish a finding, even one that is uncomfortable for a research partner. If knowing that a program was implemented poorly or didn't work as intended would cause major political challenges in your district, it may be better to conduct the analysis internally than to ask a researcher to do it. You can, however, request that the site where the research was conducted be held confidential. Anonymity may provide a more comfortable middle ground in some cases if your district will not be easily identifiable.

ADVANCED SHIFTS: SUSTAIN SUCCESS BY INVESTING MORE RESOURCES

Set a Policy of Using and Building Evidence for New Programs

You could turn rigorously pilot-testing your programs (see "Conduct a More Convincing Pilot, or Use Existing Randomization to Evaluate a Program," above) into a more advanced shift by setting a formal policy that requires staff members to build evidence any time they are testing a new program idea. A few years ago, the Wake County Public School System in North Carolina did just that. The central office asked staff proposing district projects that required new or expanded funding to describe the need the program was trying to address, the evidence that demonstrated that this was a need, the goals of the initiative, and how its effectiveness would be measured. The administration also asked staff to summarize the research that supported the proposed strategy as a way of meeting the need. This policy essentially asked staff to think through both how they knew that the proposed idea was likely to work and how they would know if it actually did work in Wake County.

A team of district staff from the offices of school performance, academics, and data and accountability then vetted these proposals. When the team thought the existing evidence was sufficiently rigorous, they would approve the request. In other cases, they met with the requestor and figured out how to launch the initiative in a way that would generate strong evidence. They even ran randomized controlled trials for some of these interventions, including an early literacy program, a program for identifying gifted students of color, and a new multitiered system of support. These studies allowed the district to learn what worked in their own situation in a more convincing way than they had previously tried and ultimately to make better decisions about whether to continue or expand these programs.

You could also approach the same idea by setting a policy of requiring a review of the evidence on multiple options when your district, department, or school is implementing new strategies, much as you might require multiple bids for a procurement. Especially when your group is considering investing substantial resources in a strategy, it's worth taking the time to carefully sort through all the evidence before settling on a plan. You could require program staff to investigate at least two options using our guiding questions and prepare a summary of the evidence for district or other group review. Consider all kinds of evidence, as we have in this book, not just the narrow definition of evidence promoted by evidence-based policy advocates. A broad-minded approach like this is exactly how districts can best take advantage of ESSA's fourth tier of evidence.

Hire a Research Director, and Let Her Direct Research

Larger districts and state agencies may have the resources to create a dedicated research director position. Carrie held a role like this in the Massachusetts Department of Elementary and Secondary Education for over a decade. When she started, she was the first research director in a state agency anywhere in the United States, and few districts had similar roles. But now it's quite common, with about half of the states and many large urban districts (and even some smaller ones) having someone on staff who spends at least part of their time on research work.

The value of a research director is that, by virtue of their being internal to the district, the person knows the district's priorities and needs. Directors are well positioned to ask questions about diagnosis, implementation, and impact and to develop strategies for answering them. They can take responsibility for implementing the bigger shifts we describe in this chapter, and they can also help with smaller things like reminding people to ask "How do we know?," supporting new routines around evidence use, and staying up-to-date on current research and sharing it with people who might find it useful.

You may feel tempted to combine research with data reporting, accountability, assessment, or other similar data-oriented roles. We strongly urge you to resist that temptation. Those roles all include intensive, sometimes time-sensitive demands for data analysis—demands that interfere with the important but not urgent work of planning for the district's needs several years down the road. If you put both types of responsibilities in the same role, the urgent will beat the important every time. These responsibilities can fall to the same organizational division or even to the same team. But at least one person (or group, in larger organizations) needs to be kept out of the fray of immediate data and reporting requests to have time to focus on longer-term work. Give your research director the space and freedom she needs to be successful. See the sidebar for a sample job description.

It can make sense, though, to couple research with strategic planning. This is a common and sensible approach, since planning will ideally include the use of research to inform district strategies and to learn from their implementation, and the learning agenda will align with the priorities that emerge from strategic planning.

If you are leading a smaller district and lack the resources to hire your own research director, you might consider working through a regional service agency or district collaborative to hire one shared across several districts. Although such a research director might have more difficulty knowing each district in depth, the

Sample Job Description for a District Research Director

Job duties include the following:

- Develop a districtwide learning agenda, and carry out the activities necessary to answer the associated research questions.
- Develop and oversee processes for managing and prioritizing requests for data, statistical analysis, and research projects from district leadership and external stakeholders, and design and carry out research that is responsive to those requests.
- Work with program staff to specify theories of action for their programs and develop implementation benchmarks and outcome measures.
- Develop rigorous qualitative and quantitative research designs for program evaluation.
- Design surveys and other data collection tools.
- Formulate and administer data-sharing agreements that help external researchers legally access confidential data to conduct research.
- Issue contracts for research work and supervise vendor activities.
- Work with program staff to apply research findings to program improvement activities.
- Communicate findings in reports, memos, and presentations.

Strong candidates will be able to demonstrate the following qualifications:

- ability to understand, interpret, and make professional judgments about complex statistical analysis and qualitative and quantitative research methodology
- prior work experience in developing and implementing a range of methodologically rigorous and sophisticated evaluation and research designs, including designs that can measure causation
- prior work experience in conducting research and applying continuous improvement methodologies in education contexts
- prior work experience in independently coordinating complex, highly visible, long-term projects with numerous stakeholders
- expertise in communicating clearly about technical material for general audiences through written and oral communications and data visualizations
- strong people and project management skills
- ability to collaborate effectively with program and research staff to achieve project results
- a master's degree or PhD in education or a related social science field

shared role has the advantage of allowing comparison, analysis, and interpretation across all participating districts to broaden and extend the learning opportunities. Another option is to assign some of these duties to a staff person, using a formal structure such as a reduction in teaching load or a stipend to recognize and compensate for the additional work.

Form a Research-Practice Partnership

If you have successfully worked with the same external research partner on a few projects, you may have reached a new level of collaboration. You and your partner might now be jointly setting your research agenda to your mutual benefit and planning for the longer term of your relationship—perhaps applying together for grants or creating a formal organizational infrastructure to support your work. If so, congratulations! You are now a member of a research-practice partnership (RPP).

RPP is an overarching term for an array of relationships between researchers and policy makers or practitioners. RPPs include the following types of partnerships:

- *Place-based alliances*, in which districts or state agencies and external research organizations collaborate to answer questions central to the district's or agency's needs.

- *Design-based partnerships*, in which partners work together to develop and test interventions, usually instructional activities or curriculum materials.

- *Networked improvement communities*, in which networks of districts aim to solve collective problems through research, often through rapid design cycles. They enable network participants to learn from what works in other settings as well as their own.[8]

RPPs are not typical research projects. An RPP is intentionally long term, mutualistic, and oriented toward solving problems of practice; it generates original analysis beyond the usual tabulations of administrative data that districts can do themselves.[9] RPPs are also distinct from situations where education leaders hire a researcher to answer a question or where researchers seek out schools or districts as sites in which to conduct studies. Neither of those relationships is long term or mutualistic.[10] Research projects can evolve into RPPs over time, however; that's how all the RPPs in Carrie's agency got their start.

The partnerships are often embedded in formal organizations such as the Chicago Consortium on School Research (the first RPP in the United States, founded in 1990). Sometimes they are housed within universities or research organizations, but this isn't a requirement. The RPPs that Carrie's agency participated in were all independent relationships without such an overarching structure. RPPs aren't so much a type of organization as they are a gestalt: a way of approaching the work of building new knowledge in practice settings.

What is the benefit of participating in an RPP instead of using a more traditional format? When executed well, RPPs solve many of the problems of integrating research with practice—problems that led us to write this book. Because the questions these partnerships investigate are mutually generated, rather than just by the researcher, the findings are more likely to be relevant to practitioners' needs and therefore more likely to be used. Research produced directly for practitioners is also more likely to result in deliverables that are accessible to practitioners and not posted behind academic publishers' paywalls. Finally, through these close collaborations, practitioners and researchers build mutual, trusting relationships that help researchers better understand the policy or practice context and help practitioners interpret the findings.

RPPs have become increasingly popular in recent years. Enough of them are up and running that there is even a National Network of Education Research-Practice Partnerships (NNERPP) to help support RPPs at all stages of development. If you are interested in pursuing this type of partnership, check out NNERPP's home page at http://nnerpp.rice.edu for resources to help you get started.

KEY TAKEAWAYS

* Everyone can make three organizational shifts to begin increasing the use of research in their organizations: (1) make research use a norm (2) increase your exposure to research, and (3) build research use into routines. These shifts take time and effort, but you can start them right now; they create crucial infrastructure for building an evidence culture.

* School districts have many options for intermediate and advanced shifts to promote and sustain the use of evidence in their organizations. A district could, for example, conduct a more convincing pilot or participate in a

research-practice partnership. Start with the shifts that you think your district is most ready for but that will challenge and stretch your thinking a bit, and build in more over time.

* If you choose to work with external researchers, hold them to high, formally established expectations. You have the data that they want; make them give you what you want in return.

APPLY YOUR LEARNING

☐ What dimensions of the three beginner shifts are you already doing, and what is new territory for your district? How could you take advantage of existing organizational routines to implement these shifts?

☐ What additional sources of evidence could you add to the materials you read or access regularly?

☐ Of the intermediate and advanced shifts, which ones feel most tractable in your district environment? What barriers do you anticipate in implementing these shifts, and how could you overcome them?

☐ How will you need to engage internal and external stakeholders to make the shifts you have prioritized?

CONCLUSION

Throughout this book, Rebecca Sisti, Maria Gonzalez, and Dwayne Taylor, the education leaders in our illustrative case studies, learned a great deal about how to use evidence to improve their work. Rebecca took on the challenge of reducing her district's chronic absenteeism rate. She and her absenteeism task force, which was led by Erin Frazier, sought out a summary of the existing research on this topic and identified a classroom greetings intervention that was appropriate in focus and scope for her district's current capacity. They then designed a system to gather information on its implementation and impact and shared the findings with their district colleagues. Maria diagnosed her problem of low eighth-grade mathematics performance by confirming that the pattern she saw on the state assessments also held true in other data. She used the five-whys protocol to analyze possible explanations. Once she settled on a strategy for improvement, she designed a way to measure whether the strategy helped, using a difference-in-differences approach that was more convincing than just a before-and-after comparison. And Dwayne spent most of his time on diagnosis. He analyzed his own available data to determine whether the complaints he'd been hearing about teacher recruitment in rural districts reflected systematic problems or squeaky wheels, so that he could develop appropriate policy responses.

The body of information these education leaders drew on—from existing research and from their own data—gave them new insights into the challenges their organization faced. Armed with this insight, they were more likely to select an appropriate strategy to solve the challenges. For Rebecca and Maria, their improved understanding also gave them a way to measure the impact of the changes they made, in a more convincing way than they might have done before. None of the analyses these leaders produced would be likely to be published in an academic journal or reviewed by the What Works Clearinghouse, much less attain its highest rating. But undeniably, all the protagonists expanded the breadth and depth of information they used in their decisions. The additional information didn't provide a silver-bullet solution, but it clearly helped move toward improvement. And each leader in his or her own way got better at leading with evidence, in a way that will help solve other problems going forward.

We began this book by advocating for the value of evidence in improving schools and districts—if evidence is viewed broadly as a way to ask and answer questions relevant for practice, not narrowly as a set of definitions and requirements that make people "do evidence." These narrow requirements are tempting from a policy perspective but are ultimately limiting because they exclude too many questions and answers that are crucial for the real work of educational improvement.

Our goal was to show you how to use evidence in the real world. Now you're equipped to ask questions about impact, and also important questions about diagnosing problems and implementing strategies to solve them. You've learned to quickly separate the wheat from the chaff of educational research so that you can focus on the most relevant, convincing evidence for your needs. And hopefully you've come to appreciate the importance of building your own evidence base. Now you know how to conduct useful comparisons and analyses to learn from, and improve, your work. You can interpret and share your results through examples, writing, and data visualizations. And you've examined many ways to embed the use of more evidence into your organizational routines, so that it becomes part of business as usual.

As the field of education advances, educators will continue to ask new questions, generate new sources of data, and solve new problems. And as the field of research advances, researchers will continue to find answers to new questions and to develop new methodologies for answering them. Though the forefront of the work is always a moving target, the tools for asking better questions and determining whether the answers are relevant and convincing—the tools of this book—are unchanging.

We hope you will take advantage of the new tools in your toolkit to ask questions that promote better and more equitable outcomes, choose strategies that have a basis in evidence where you can, and evaluate their implementation and impact so that you can improve your work over time. As with any other tools, as you use these more often, you will become more proficient. We also hope you will pass on what you learn from this book with your colleagues near and far, whether through formal structures like conference presentations and professional publications or informally through real and virtual social networks. Please share your success stories and challenges with us on Twitter at @NoraEGordon and @clconaway using the hashtag #CommonSenseEvidence, so that we can build a community of educators dedicated to greater use of evidence in education policy and practice.

Most of all, we hope you are convinced that it doesn't take years of statistical training or fancy research methods to use evidence well. It just takes asking good questions, making smart comparisons, and using common sense.

FURTHER READINGS

Importance of Evidence

Brekton, Jonathan. *Using Research Evidence: A Practice Guide*. London: Nesta, n.d. http://wtgrantfoundation.org/library/uploads/2018/07/Using-Research-Evidence-for-Success-A-Practice-Guide-v6-web.pdf.

Willingham, Daniel. *When Can You Trust the Experts? How to Tell Good Science from Bad in Education*. San Francisco: Jossey-Bass, 2012.

Statistics and Research Methods (roughly ordered from least to most technical)

Kille, Leighton Walter. "Statistical Terms Used in Research Studies: a Primer for Media." *Journalist's Resource*, April 7, 2015. https://journalistsresource.org/tip-sheets/research/statistics-for-journalists.

Stigler, Stephen M. *The Seven Pillars of Statistical Wisdom*. Cambridge, MA: Harvard University Press, 2016.

Wheelan, Charles. *Naked Statistics: Stripping the Dread from the Data*. New York: W.W. Norton & Company, 2013.

Loeb, Susanna, Susan Dynarski, Daniel McFarland, Pamela Morris, Sean Reardon, and Sarah Reber. *Descriptive Analysis in Education: A Guide for Researchers*. Washington, DC: US Department of Education, Institute of Education Sciences, National Center for Education Evaluation and Regional Assistance, 2017.

Remler, Dahlia K., and Gregg G. Van Ryzin. *Research Methods in Practice: Strategies for Description and Causation*. Los Angeles: Sage Publications, 2015.

Murnane, Richard J., and John B. Willett. *Methods Matter: Improving Causal Inference in Educational and Social Science Research*. New York: Oxford University Press, 2011.

Data Use for School Improvement

Boudett, Kathryn Parker, Elizabeth A. City, and Richard J. Murnane, eds. *Data Wise: A Step-by-Step Guide to Using Assessment Results to Improve Teaching and Learning*. Cambridge, MA: Harvard Education Press, 2017.

Bryk, Anthony S., Louis M. Gomez, Alicia Grunow, and Paul G. LeMahieu. *Learning to Improve: How America's Schools Can Get Better at Getting Better*. Cambridge, MA: Harvard Education Press, 2017.

Writing Skills

Dreyer, Benjamin. *Dreyer's English: An Utterly Correct Guide to Clarity and Style*. New York: Random House, 2019.

McCloskey, Deirdre. *Economical Writing: Thirty-Five Rules for Clear and Persuasive Prose*. Chicago: University of Chicago Press, 2019.

Miller, Jane E. *The Chicago Guide to Writing About Numbers*. Chicago: University of Chicago Press, 2015.

Zinsser, William. *On Writing Well: The Classic Guide to Writing Nonfiction*. New York: Harper Perennial, 2006.

Data Displays

Few, Stephen. *Show Me the Numbers: Designing Tables and Graphs to Enlighten*. Oakland, CA: Analytics Press, 2004.

Tufte, Edward. *The Visual Display of Quantitative Information*. Cheshire, CT: Graphics Press, 2001.

Wong, Dona M. *The Wall Street Journal Guide to Information Graphics: The Dos and Don'ts of Presenting Data, Facts, and Figures*. New York: W.W. Norton & Company, 2013.

Other Useful Resources

Heath, Chip, and Dan Heath. *Made to Stick: Why Some Ideas Take Hold and Others Come Unstuck*. Arrow Books, 2007.

Pew Research Center. "Questionnaire Design." 2019. https://www.pewresearch.org/methods/u-s-survey-research/questionnaire-design.

NOTES

Introduction

1. William R. Penuel et al., "Findings from a National Study on Research Use Among School and District Leaders," *National Center for Research in Policy and Practice*, no. 1 (April 2016): 55.

2. Robert Slavin, "Programs and Practices," *Robert Slavin's Blog*, August 23, 2018, https:// robertslavinsblog.wordpress.com/2018/08/23/programs-and-practices.

3. Brian A. Jacob and Jonah E. Rockoff, "Organizing Schools to Improve Student Achievement: Start Times, Grade Configurations, and Teacher Assignments," Brookings Institution discussion paper 2011-08 (Brookings Institution: September 2011), 28.

4. Carol H. Weiss, "Policy Research in the Context of Diffuse Decision Making," *Journal of Higher Education* 53, no. 6 (1982): 619–39, https://doi.org/10.2307/1981522.

5. Weiss, "Policy Research"; Caitlin Farrell and Cynthia E. Coburn, "What Is the Conceptual Use of Research, and Why Is It Important?," William T. Grant Foundation, April 8, 2016, http://wtgrantfoundation.org/conceptual-use-research-important.

6. Daniel Kahneman, *Thinking Fast and Slow* (New York: Farrar, Straus and Giroux, 2011).

7. Gerald J. Langley et al., *The Improvement Guide: A Practical Approach to Enhancing Organizational Performance*, 2nd ed. (San Francisco: Jossey-Bass, 2009); Kathryn Parker Boudett, Elizabeth A. City, and Richard J. Murnane, *Data Wise: A Step-by-Step Guide to Using Assessment Results to Improve Teaching and Learning* (Cambridge, MA: Harvard Education Press, 2013); Anthony S. Bryk et al., *Learning to Improve: How America's Schools Can Get Better at Getting Better* (Cambridge, MA: Harvard Education Press, 2015).

Chapter 1

1. Fred Wulczyn, Lily Alpert, and Britany Orlebeke, "Principles, Language, and Shared Meaning: Toward a Common Understanding of CQI in Child Welfare," Center for State Child Welfare Data, Chapin Hall at the University of Chicago, July 2014, https:// www.chapinhall.org/wp-content/uploads/2014-07-Principles-Language-and-Shared -Meaning_Toward-a-Common-Understanding-of-CQI-in-Child-Welfare.pdf.

2. "The How Do We Know Initiative," Office of Planning and Research, Massachusetts Department of Elementary and Secondary Education, http://www.doe.mass.edu/research/howdoweknow.

3. Frederick Hess, *Cage-Busting Leadership* (Cambridge, MA: Harvard Education Press, 2013).

4. Taiichi Ohno, *Toyota Production System: Beyond Large-Scale Production* (Cambridge, MA: Productivity Press, 1988).

5. "Elementary and Secondary Education Act of 1965," ESSA Sec. 8101 (21)(A), https://www2.ed.gov/documents/essa-act-of-1965.pdf

6. David Blazar et al., "Learning by the Book: Comparing Math Achievement Growth by Textbook in Six Common Core States," Center for Education Policy Research, Harvard University, March 2019.

7. Center for Benefit-Cost Studies of Education (CBCSE), "CostOut," CBCSE, Teachers College Columbia University, https://www.cbcse.org/costout.

8. Melissa Junge and Sheara Krvaric, "How Confusion over Federal Rules Can Get in the Way of Smart School Spending," American Enterprise Institute, December 2019, https://www.aei.org/wp-content/uploads/2019/11/How-Confusion-over-Federal-Rules-Can-Get-in-the-Way-of-Smart-School-Spending.pdf.

9. "The Massachusetts Planning and Implementation Framework: Multi-Year Plan Components," Massachusetts Department of Elementary and Secondary Education, http://www.doe.mass.edu/research/success/implementation-framework.docx.

Chapter 2

1. Jonathan D. Schoenfeld and John PA Ioannidis, "Is Everything We Eat Associated with Cancer? A Systematic Cookbook Review," *American Journal of Clinical Nutrition* 97, no. 1 (2013): 127–34, https://doi.org/10.3945/ajcn.112.047142.

2. A search for "chronic absenteeism" and "chronic absence" on the WWC practice guides and intervention reports on September 12, 2019, returned no results. A search for "attendance" on the same day returned seven results, all of which focused on dropout prevention with a focus on middle and high school students. About two months later, on November 9, 2019, a search for "chronic absenteeism" on the Campbell Collaboration website returned one result about how truancy programs improve attendance. The same day, a search for "chronic absence" returned the same result and a search for "truancy" returned six results, only two of which were relevant to truancy interventions. While one of these results was a review of truancy intervention programs, some of which included elementary students, the authors note that studies focusing specifically on interventions aimed at elementary students were lacking.

3. Evie Blad, "ESSA Puts Pressure on Schools to Reduce Student Absences; Here's How They Might Do It," *Education Week*, August 4, 2019, http://blogs.edweek.org/edweek/campaign-k-12/2019/08/essa-chronic-absenteeism-evidence-based.html.

4. Phyllis Jordan, "Attendance Playbook: Smart Solutions for Reducing Chronic Absenteeism," FutureEd, Georgetown University, July 2019, https://www.future-ed.org/wp-content/uploads/2019/07/Attendance-Playbook.pdf.

5. Denise-Marie Ordway, "The Literature Review and Meta-Analysis: 2 Journalism Tools You Should Use," *Journalist's Resource*, June 20, 2019, https://journalistsresource.org/tip-sheets/research/meta-analysis-literature-review.

6. Rachael Gabriel, "Is the Research Trustworthy? Learn to Think Like an Investigator," *ASCD Express*, August 22, 2019, http://www.ascd.org/ascd-express/vol14/num34/is-the-research-trustworthy-learn-to-think-like-an-investigator.aspx.

7. Margaret E. Goertz, Leslie Nabors Olah, and Matthew Riggan, *From Testing to Teaching: The Use of Interim Assessments in Classroom Instruction*, research report RR-65 (Consortium for Policy Research in Education, December 2009), https://repository.upenn.edu/cgi/viewcontent.cgi?article=1023&context=cpre_researchreports.

8. L. S. Hall, "More Funding Is Flowing for Education Journalism; Is That OK?," *Inside Philanthropy*, July 21, 2015, https://www.insidephilanthropy.com/home/2015/7/21/more-funding-is-flowing-for-education-journalism-is-that-ok.html.

9. William R. Penuel et al., "Findings from a National Study on Research Use Among School and District Leaders," *National Center for Research in Policy and Practice*, no. 1 (April 2016): 55.

10. David Trilling, "Writing About Think Tanks and Using Their Research: A Cautionary Tip Sheet," *Journalist's Resource*, March 6, 2017, https://journalistsresource.org/tip-sheets/think-tanks-writing-research-journalists.

11. Jordan, "Attendance Playbook." Disclaimer: Nora is a member of the advisory board of FutureEd. She is not paid for her services.

12. Penuel et al., "National Study on Research Use."

13. Ian Larkin, Desmond Ang, Jonathan Steinhart, Matthew Chao, Mark Patterson, Sunita Sah, Tina Wu, Michael Schoenbaum, David Hutchins, Troyen Brennan, and George Loewenstein, "Association Between Academic Medical Center Pharmaceutical Detailing Policies and Physician Prescribing," *Journal of the American Medical Association* 317, no. 17 (2017): 1785–95, https://jamanetwork.com/journals/jama/fullarticle/2623607.

14. Disclaimer: Usable Knowledge (http://gse.harvard.edu/uk/) is a site of the Harvard Graduate School of Education, where Carrie is a senior lecturer. Nora is a member of the Scholars Strategy Network (https://scholars.org). The Conversation home page can be found at https://theconversation.com/us.

15. Institute of Education Sciences, "The Regional Educational Laboratory Program (REL): About Us," https://ies.ed.gov/ncee/edlabs/about.

16. researchED, "About Us," https://researched.org.uk/about.

17. "Making Connections with Greetings at the Door," *Edutopia*, January 14, 2019, https://www.edutopia.org/video/making-connections-greetings-door.

18. As of September 19, 2019, Edutopia had 1,367,850 followers on Facebook (https://www.facebook.com/edutopia/) and 108,000 subscribers on YouTube (https://www.youtube.com/edutopia).

19. "First Ever Free Consumer Reports-Style Review of Instructional Materials Released," *EdReports*, March 4, 2015, https://www.edreports.org/resources/article/first-ever-free-consumer-reports-style-review-of-instructional-materials-released.

Chapter 3

1. Phyllis Jordan, "Attendance Playbook: Smart Solutions for Reducing Chronic Absenteeism," FutureEd, Georgetown University, July 2019, https://www.future-ed.org/wp-content/uploads/2019/07/Attendance-Playbook.pdf.

2. Clayton R. Cook et al., "Positive Greetings at the Door: Evaluation of a Low-Cost, High-Yield Proactive Classroom Management Strategy," *Journal of Positive Behavior Interventions* 20, no. 3 (July 1, 2018): 149–59, https://doi.org/10.1177/1098300717753831.

3. Cook et al., "Positive Greetings at the Door."

4. What Works Clearinghouse, "Success for All®," Institute of Education Sciences, US Department of Education August 2009), https://ies.ed.gov/ncee/wwc/Docs/InterventionReports/wwc_sfa_081109.pdf.

5. Jordan, "Attendance Playbook."

6. Cook et al., "Positive Greetings at the Door."

7. Katherine Michelmore and Susan Dynarski, "The Gap Within the Gap: Using Longitudinal Data to Understand Income Differences in Educational Outcomes," *AERA Open* 3, no. 1 (2017): 1–18.

8. Erica Greenberg, Kristin Blagg, and Macy Rainer, "Measuring Student Poverty: Developing Accurate Counts for School Funding, Accountability, and Research," Urban Institute, December 2019, https://www.urban.org/sites/default/files/publication/101430/measuring_student_poverty.pdf.

9. Cook et al., "Positive Greetings at the Door."

10. Youki Terada, "Welcoming Students with a Smile," *Edutopia*, September 11, 2018, https://www.edutopia.org/article/welcoming-students-smile.

11. Elizabeth A. Stuart et al., "Characteristics of School Districts That Participate in Rigorous National Educational Evaluations," *Journal of Research on Educational Effectiveness* 10, no. 1 (2017): 168–206, https://doi.org/10.1080/19345747.2016.1205160.

12. Ellen Condliffe Lagemann, *An Elusive Science: The Troubling History of Education Research* (Chicago: University of Chicago Press, 2000).

13. Jeanna Smialek, "Nobel Economics Prize Goes to Pioneers in Reducing Poverty," *New York Times*, October 14, 2019, https://www.nytimes.com/2019/10/14/business/nobel -economics.html; Esther Duflo, *Social Experiments to Fight Poverty*, TED talk, video and transcript, February 2010, https://www.ted.com/talks/esther_duflo_social _experiments_to_fight_poverty.

14. For an example using such a rule (maximum class size in Israel of 40), see: Joshua D. Angrist and Victor Lavy, "Using Maimonides' Rule to Estimate the Effect of Class Size on Scholastic Achievement," *Quarterly Journal of Economics* (1999): 533–75.

15. Kathryn Van Eck et al., "How School Climate Relates to Chronic Absence: A Multi- Level Latent Profile Analysis," *Journal of School Psychology* 61 (2017): 89–102.

16. Jordan, "Attendance Playbook."

17. For a slightly more detailed description, see Chloe Reichel, "Statistics for Journalists: Understanding What Effect Size Means," *Journalist's Resource*, June 25, 2019, https:// journalistsresource.org/tip-sheets/research/effect-size-statistics-risk-ratio.

18. John Hattie, *Visible Learning: A Synthesis of Over 800 Meta-Analyses Relating to Achieve- ment* (New York: Routledge, 2009), 4. John Hattie, "Hattie Ranking: 252 Influences and Effect Sizes Related to Achievement," *Visible Learning*, December 2017, https://visible -learning.org/hattie-ranking-influences-effect-sizes-learning-achievement.

19. Kraft, Matthew A. "Interpreting Effect Sizes of Education Interventions." *Educational Researcher*, April 2020, doi:10.3102/0013189X20912798.

20. Kraft, "Effect Sizes of Education Interventions."

21. Denise-Marie Ordway, Debra Viadero, and Holly Yettick, "Making Sense of Education Research," Education Writers Association, https://www.ewa.org/education-research. See the free Reporter Guides on Education Research from the Education Writers of America at https://www.ewa.org/education-research for more such user-friendly writ- ing about research.

22. See, for example, Regina Nuzzo, "Scientific Method: Statistical Errors," *Nature*, Febru- ary 12, 2014, https://www.nature.com/news/scientific-method-statistical-errors -1.14700; Valentin Amrhein, Sander Greenland, and Blake McShane, "Scientists Rise Up against Statistical Significance," *Nature*, March 20, 2019 305–7, https://doi.org /10.1038/d41586-019-00857-9; Ron Wasserstein, "American Statistical Association Releases Statement on Statistical Significance and P-Values," American Statistical Association, March 7, 2016, https://www.amstat.org/asa/files/pdfs/P-ValueStatement. pdf; American Economic Association, "AEA Papers and Proceedings Guidelines," American Economic Association, https://www.aeaweb.org/journals/pandp/styleguide; and Carrie Conaway and Dan Goldhaber, "Appropriate Standards of Evidence for

Education Policy Decision-Making," *Education Finance and Policy*, September 18, 2019, 1–22, https://doi.org/10.1162/edfp_a_00301.

Chapter 4

1. For a scholarly legal explanation of these requirements, see Eloise Pasachoff, "Two Cheers for Evidence: Law, Research, and Values in Education Policymaking and Beyond," *Columbia Law Review* 117, no. 7 (2017), https://columbialawreview.org /content/two-cheers-for-evidence-law-research-and-values-in-education-policy making-and-beyond.

2. "Non-Regulatory Guidance: Using Evidence to Strengthen Education Investments," Guidance Document, US Department of Education, September 16, 2016, https:// www2.ed.gov/policy/elsec/leg/essa/guidanceuseseinvestment.pdf.

3. "Non-Regulatory Guidance."

4. "Non-Regulatory Guidance."

5. "Non-Regulatory Guidance."

6. Carrie Conaway, "Tier 4 Evidence: ESSA's Hidden Gem," *Phi Delta Kappan*, May 3, 2018, https://www.kappanonline.org/conaway-tier-4-evidence-essas-hidden-gem.

7. Deans for Impact, "The Science of Learning," Deans for Impact, Austin, TX, 2015, https://deansforimpact.org/wp-content/uploads/2016/12/The_Science_of_Learning.pdf.

8. John Sweller, "Cognitive Load During Problem Solving: Effects on Learning," *Cognitive Science* 12, no. 2 (1988): 257–85, https://doi.org/10.1016/0364-0213(88)90023-7.

9. Fabio Richlan, Martin Kronbichler, and Heinz Wimmer, "Meta-Analyzing Brain Dysfunctions in Dyslexic Children and Adults," *NeuroImage* 56, no. 3 (2011): 1735–42, https://doi.org/10.1016/j.neuroimage.2011.02.040; Fabio Richlan, Martin Kronbichler, and Heinz Wimmer, "Structural Abnormalities in the Dyslexic Brain: A Meta-Analysis of Voxel-Based Morphometry Studies," *Human Brain Mapping* 34, no. 11 (2013): 3055–65, https://doi.org/10.1002/hbm.22127.

10. Robert F. Anda et al., "The Enduring Effects of Abuse and Related Adverse Experiences in Childhood," *European Archives of Psychiatry and Clinical Neuroscience* 256, no. 3 (2006): 174–86, https://doi.org/10.1007/s00406-005-0624-4.

11. Michele Lamont and Patricia White, "Workshop on Interdisciplinary Standards for Systematic Qualitative Research," National Science Foundation, 2005, https://www.nsf .gov/sbe/ses/soc/ISSQR_rpt.pdf; Charles C. Ragin, Joane Nagel, and Patricia White, "Workshop on Scientific Foundations of Qualitative Research," National Science Foundation, 2004, https://www.nsf.gov/pubs/2004/nsf04219/nsf04219.pdf.

12. Carolyn Sattin-Bajaj et al., "Surviving at the Street Level: How Counselors' Implementation of School Choice Policy Shapes Students' High School Destinations," *American Sociological Association* 91, no. 1 (2018): 46–71.

13. Carolyn J. Heinrich et al., "A Look Inside Online Educational Settings in High School: Promise and Pitfalls for Improving Educational Opportunities and Outcomes," *American Educational Research Journal* 56, no. 6 (March 27, 2019), https://doi.org /10.3102/0002831219838776.

Chapter 5

1. Massachusetts Department of Elementary and Secondary Education, "District Analysis and Review Tool (DART)," http://profiles.doe.mass.edu/analysis/state.aspx.
2. For example, see Anne Podolsky et al., "California's Positive Outliers: Districts Beating the Odds," *Learning Policy Institute*, May 2019, 8.
3. For the purpose of this example, we are assuming that the state testing system generates a scaled score that runs from 200 to 300 and is designed to allow fair comparisons of scaled scores across years, grades, and subjects. This is not always the case. You should be careful to read up on the appropriate uses and limitations of any data you obtain from an assessment system before using it to evaluate a program. See the section titled "Assessment Data" later in this chapter.
4. Podolsky et al., "California's Positive Outliers."
5. Leah Shafer, "When Proficient Isn't Good," *Usable Knowledge* (Harvard Graduate School of Education), January 4, 2016, https://www.gse.harvard.edu/news/uk/15/12 /when-proficient-isnt-good.
6. Kathryn Parker Boudett, Elizabeth A. City, and Richard J. Murnane, eds., *Data Wise: A Step-by-Step Guide to Using Assessment Results to Improve Teaching and Learning* (Cambridge, MA: Harvard Education Press, 2017).
7. Hunter Gehlbach and Anthony Artino Jr., "The Survey Checklist (Manifesto)," *Academic Medicine* 93, no. 3 (2018): 360–66.
8. Pew Research Center, "Questionnaire Design," https://www.pewresearch.org/methods /u-s-survey-research/questionnaire-design.
9. Angela L. Duckworth and David Scott Yeager, "Measurement Matters: Assessing Personal Qualities Other Than Cognitive Ability for Educational Purposes," *Educational Researcher*, 44, no. 4 (2015), https://doi.org/10.3102/0013189X15584327.

Chapter 6

1. Jacob Cohen, *Statistical Power Analysis for the Behavioral Sciences*, (New York: Academic Press, 1969).
2. Kraft, Matthew A. "Interpreting Effect Sizes of Education Interventions." *Educational Researcher*, April 2020, doi:10.3102/0013189X20912798.
3. Chip Heath and Dan Heath, *Made to Stick: Why Some Ideas Survive and Others Die* (New York: Random House, 2008).

4. Stephen Few, *Show Me the Numbers: Designing Tables and Graphs to Enlighten* (Oakland, CA: Analytics Press, 2004).

5. Stephen Few, "Data Visualization for Human Perception," in *The Encyclopedia of Human-Computer Interaction*, ed. Claude Ghaoui (Hershey, PA: Idea Group Reference, 2006), https://www.interaction-design.org/literature/book/the-encyclopedia -of-human-computer-interaction-2nd-ed/data-visualization-for-human-perception.

6. Stephen Few, "Save the Pies for Dessert," *Perceptual Edge: Visual Business Intelligence Newsletter*, August 2007. https://www.perceptualedge.com/articles/visual_business _intelligence/save_the_pies_for_dessert.pdf.

Chapter 7

1. Kathryn Parker Boudett and Meghan Lockwood, "The Power of Team Norms," *Educational Leadership*, ASCD, July 2019, http://www.ascd.org/publications/educational -leadership/jul19/vol76/num09/The-Power-of-Team-Norms.aspx.

2. Boudett and Lockwood, "The Power of Team Norms."

3. Laura Booker, Carrie Conaway, and Nate Schwartz, "Five Ways RPPs Can Fail and How to Avoid Them: Applying Conceptual Frameworks to Improve RPPs," William T. Grant Foundation, May 2019, 18, http://wtgrantfoundation.org/library/uploads/2019 /06/Five-Ways-RPPs-Can-Fail.pdf.

4. Booker, Conaway, and Schwartz, "Five Ways RPPs Can Fail."

5. US Department of Education, "Written Agreement Checklist," 2012, 4, https://student privacy.ed.gov/resources/written-agreement-checklist.

6. "Family Educational Rights and Privacy Act Regulations," 34 CFR Part 99 § (2009), https://www2.ed.gov/policy/gen/guid/fpco/pdf/ferparegs.pdf.

7. American Association of University Professors, "1940 Statement of Principles on Academic Freedom and Tenure, with 1970 Interpretive Comments," https://www.aaup.org /report/1940-statement-principles-academic-freedom-and-tenure.

8. Cynthia E. Coburn, William R. Penuel, and Kimberly E. Geil, "Research-Practice Partnerships: A Strategy for Leveraging Research for Educational Improvement in School Districts," William T. Grant Foundation, January 2013, http://wtgrantfoundation.org /library/uploads/2015/10/Research-Practice-Partnerships-at-the-District-Level.pdf.

9. Cynthia E. Coburn and William R. Penuel, "Research-Practice Partnerships in Education: Outcomes, Dynamics, and Open Questions," *Educational Researcher*, January 1, 2016, https://doi.org/10.3102/0013189X16631750; William R. Penuel and Daniel J. Gallagher, *Creating Research-Practice Partnerships in Education* (Cambridge, MA: Harvard Education Press, 2017).

10. Penuel and Gallagher, *Research-Practice Partnerships in Education*.

ACKNOWLEDGMENTS

This book is a result of decades of relationships and conversations with our colleagues, with those who taught us and those we've taught, with education leaders and practitioners, and with policy makers, advocates, and journalists. We are grateful for the opportunity to learn from and with so many people, only a few of whom are named here.

We have benefited from feedback on various drafts from a stellar group of researchers and education leaders, none of whom are responsible for any of our errors. Karla Baehr, Matt Kraft, Bob Lee, and Richard Murnane went above and beyond in their generosity of time and expertise. We also owe thanks to Sarah Cohodes, Liz Farley-Ripple, Andrew Ho, Robin Jacob, Melissa Junge, Sarah Reber, Nate Schwartz, Josh Starr, Leanna Steifel, Brenda Turnbull, and Julie Wilson for their thoughtful suggestions.

Conversations with many colleagues helped shape our thinking and build the examples we draw on in the book. This is surely a partial list: Lily Alpert, Kathryn Parker Boudett, Lauren Camera, Ethan Cancell, Jill Clark, Caitlin Farrell, Steve Fleischman, Dan Goldhaber, Michael Gottfried, Carolyn Hill, Darryl Hill, Melissa Junge, Eric Kalenze, Sara Kerr, Jacob Kirsey, Karen Kleiber, Sheara Krvaric, Jonathan Ladd, Matt Lenard, Joy Lesnick, Lori Likis, Antoniya Marinova, Michele McLaughlin, Ruth Curran Neild, Alexandra Pardo, Eloise Pasachoff, Eva Rosen, Sonja Santelises, Elizabeth Stuart, Vivian Tseng, Bi Vuong, and Russ Whitehurst. We benefited from early feedback on some core concepts from the State Education Fellows network convened by Results for America and from Carrie's staff at the Massachusetts Department of Elementary and Secondary Education.

We are grateful to Caroline Chauncey, our editor at Harvard Education Press, for her generous support and positivity through multiple rounds of proposals and drafts. The book is far better for her expertise, good judgment, and constructive suggestions. Patricia Boyd, our exceptional copyeditor, eliminated errors, ambiguity, and many extra words; we are beyond grateful. Our fantastic research assistants tracked down citations, conducted statistical analyses, provided feedback on our writing, and helped us develop our case examples. Thank you, Omolara Fatiregun, Krista O'Connell, Linda Rosenbury, Jill Da Eun Seong, and Kennedy Weisner.

Finally, Twitter's virtual community has broadened our perspectives. It's inspiring to know how many people we don't know in real life are working so hard to help students and to share their experiences with the world. We hope this book helps many of you.

From Nora

I am grateful to George Akerlof, Phil Cooke, and Melissa Kearney for suggesting the radical idea of a book, and to Rick Hess and Carole Sargent for guiding me through the process.

I was lucky to write this book during a year of sabbatical leave, supported by Georgetown University. Dave Marcotte and American University's School of Public Affairs generously provided a sabbatical home, complete with welcoming colleagues and stimulating conversation.

To my colleagues and especially my students at Georgetown University's McCourt School of Public Policy, thank you for engaging so fully. You have pushed me to crystallize my thinking about what does and doesn't matter when applying research to practice and policy. Without your perspectives and skepticism, this book wouldn't exist.

It has meant so much that my family and friends asked how the writing was going, showed interest in the topic, and, most of all, believed that this book would get written. My parents, Laura Kramer and Bill Gordon, were my original teachers of common sense. I'm grateful for their unconditional love and support. And Mom, thanks for reading the final manuscript. John Douard, Betty Ferber, Joanna Gordon, Zoe Gordon, Suzanne Horowitz, Tom Rebbeck, Jessica Williams, and Mark Williams—thank you for supporting our family. I miss my father-in-law Leonard Horowitz and my dear friend Bob Pomerance. I know they would have read this entire book despite its irrelevance to their professional lives, which says it all about their love and devotion. To Johana Gonzalez, I am so thankful that you care not only for my children and home but also for me.

My children, Gabe, Zach, and Aaron Horowitz, are my greatest pride and my greatest cheerleaders. To my husband Jeremy Horowitz, who has supported me unfailingly, from taking a red pen to the proposal to protecting my time and raising my spirits through the last word: even those times when I was too preoccupied to thank you, I noticed, and I am grateful.

From Carrie

In my career as a researcher in a government agency, I benefited from nearly a decade of mentorship from Mitchell Chester, the former commissioner of elementary and secondary education in Massachusetts, who died in 2017. He demonstrated every day what leading with evidence looks like. I also benefited from the opportunity to work with and learn from my colleagues at the Massachusetts Department of Elementary and Secondary Education. They are the best in the business when it comes to using research to improve education policy. I could not have written this book without those experiences. My new colleagues at the Harvard Graduate School of Education welcomed me warmly when I left my state position in the summer of 2019. Thank you in particular to Dean Bridget Terry Long for believing in my potential to contribute to the community and giving me the gift of time to work on this project.

I am grateful for my friendships with Nyal Fuentes and Bob Lee, who provided encouragement, a good laugh, or a ribbing whenever one was needed. My weightlifting coaches Ellyn Robinson and Lorie Blair and my Robinson Weightlifting teammates provided much-needed structure, balance, and social interaction throughout a challenging year. I also thank Dr. Michael Lechnar, my high school history teacher, who opened my eyes to the world of the social sciences and set me on the path toward my career.

I wish my parents, Mary and Dennis Conaway, could have lived long enough to see me join the Harvard faculty and write a book in the same year. I know they would have been so proud of my accomplishments. But I am thrilled that I can share my successes with my sister Christie Olvera, brother-in-law Adrian Olvera Campos, and their children Artemio, Arquimedes, Amadeus, and Azalea. Most importantly, I couldn't be more grateful to my husband Maxim Weinstein. All that *Free to Be . . . You and Me* as a kid must have worked, because he never wavered in his encouragement of my ambitions or his belief in my abilities. He provided support both moral and technical, and he covered the home front on many evenings and weekends while I was writing. Without Max, I would gripe more and laugh less.

From both of us

Writing this book has somehow been simultaneously exhilarating, challenging, and tedious. It required energy, expertise, and devotion from both of us to come to life, and neither one of us could have written it alone. We want to thank each other for her friendship, intellectual partnership, and common sense.

ABOUT THE AUTHORS

NORA GORDON is an associate professor at the McCourt School of Public Policy at Georgetown University. She also is a research associate of the National Bureau of Economic Research, a nonresident fellow of the Urban Institute, a member of the Professional Advisory Board of the National Center for Learning Disabilities, and an associate editor of the journal *Education Finance and Policy*. Her research examines how education policy affects equity. In addition to publishing her own research on school finance and other equity-related topics in academic journals, she enjoys writing for popular audiences. She has written for the *New York Times*, *Education Week*, and www.TheAtlantic.com; has been interviewed on NPR a number of times; and was a regular contributor to the *Evidence Speaks* blog at the Brookings Institution. Dr. Gordon has testified before Congress on the implementation of the Every Student Succeeds Act and served on the Institute of Education Sciences expert panel on the Study of the Title I Formula. She earned her PhD in economics from Harvard University and her BA in economics from Swarthmore College.

CARRIE CONAWAY is a senior lecturer on education at the Harvard Graduate School of Education, where she teaches students how to use evidence to improve organizations and how to interpret data effectively—the same skills covered in this book. Until June 2019, she was the research and planning director for the Massachusetts Department of Elementary and Secondary Education, the first research director in a state education agency in the nation. During her twelve years there, she commissioned over two hundred studies and developed five research-practice partnerships to help the agency improve its work. She received the Commonwealth of Massachusetts Workforce Mentoring Award in 2014. Before her state service, she was a journalist and the deputy director of a research center on regional economic policy. In 2018, she was elected president of the Association for Education Finance and Policy, a national association of education policy researchers. She writes frequently in peer-reviewed and general-audience publications on the use of research in education policy. She earned her MA in sociology from Harvard University, her MA in public affairs from the University of Minnesota, and her BA in sociology from Oberlin College.

▪   ▪   ▪

Gordon and Conaway met as graduate students in the Harvard Kennedy School's Multidisciplinary Program on Inequality & Social Policy and have enjoyed discussing the mysterious shortage of common sense in education research, public policy, and academia ever since.

INDEX

A

absenteeism example
  audience considerations, 120–121
  combining data comparisons, 98–101
  communicating evidence, 113
  comparisons of data, 88–95, 119, 121–122
  continuing culture of evidence after, 137–138
  data, 85–86
  data displays, 127–130
  defining the problem, 12
  diagnosing a problem, 18
  draft findings, 118
  evaluating causation versus correlation, 60–61
  evaluating existing research, 49
  evaluating relevance, 53, 54, 56, 57
  evaluating statistical significance, 67–68
  finding existing research, 33, 39–40, 41
  impact evaluation questions, 26
  learning agenda, 144–146
  outliers in data, 105–106
  overall presentation structure, 131–134
  pilot tests, 141
  process measures, 25
  scatterplots and regression analysis, 101–104
  simplifying data, 85–87
  titles for data displays, 126–127
abstracts, 36, 37
academic journals, 30–31, 37, 40, 44
academic performance example
  combining data comparisons, 95–98
  commitment to action in advance, 143–144
  diagnosing a problem, 15
  finding existing research, 33, 36–37
  impact evaluation questions, 26
  implementation strategy, 24
academic research
  overviews of, 34–35
  sources of, 35–37

advocacy groups, 39–40
arbitrary selection, 62–63
assessment data, 106–108
association size, 65, 119. *see also* effect size
assumptions, questioning, 11, 86, 140–141
audience considerations, for communicating
  evidence, 115–116, 120–121
authors of studies. *see* researchers
average (mean), 86

B

bar charts, 124, 127–128. *see also* data displays
basic research, 80–81
bias. *see* cognitive bias; selection bias

C

Campbell Collaboration, 31
causation (cause and effect)
  arbitrary selection affecting, 62–63
  effect size affecting, 65–66
  ESSA criteria for, 74
  language claiming, 64–65
  RCTs affecting, 61–62
  selection bias affecting, 60–65, 68–69
Chalkbeat, 38
charts. *see* data displays
choice-based high school example, 81–82
citations, 36, 44, 45
cognitive bias
  of audience, 116
  of researchers, 30
  your own, addressing, 4, 11, 15, 143
Cohen's *d* statistic. *see* effect size
communicating evidence
  audience considerations, 115–116, 120
  concrete example for, 117
  data comparisons for, 120–122
  data displays for. *see* data displays

communicating evidence, *continued*
  findings, writing, 117–122
  most powerful evidence, identifying,
    114–117
  overall presentation for, 131–134
  technical language usage in, 122
comparisons of data
  combining, 95–101
  in findings, 120–122
  with goals, 88–89
  between observations, 92–95
  over time, 90–92, 98–99
confidence interval, 66, 68–69
confidentiality, 150–151, 152
confounders. *see* control variables; selection
    bias
continuous improvement systems, 6, 85
control variables
  definition of, 55
  ESSA promising evidence requiring, 76, 78
  finding in studies, 51, 63
Conversation, 40
convincingness of research
  criteria for, 47, 68–69
  evaluating based on causation versus correla-
    tion, 59–66
  evaluating based on statistical significance,
    66–68, 68–69
  objective perspective for, 48
correlation versus causation, 59–66
costs, for implementation of strategy, 22–24
criterion-referenced scores, 107
culture of evidence use
  advanced level of, 153–158
  beginning level of, 139–141
  commitment to action in advance, 143–144
  existing routines, adding evidence use to,
    137–140
  external researchers, working with,
    149–152
  intermediate level of, 141–152
  learning agenda, creating, 144–149
  organizational norms for, 140–141
  pilot tests, conducting, 141–143
  requiring new programs to build evidence,
    153
  research director, hiring, 154–156

research-practice partnerships (RPPs) for,
    156–157
sources of research, increasing exposure to,
    139

D
data. *see also* evidence
  assessment data, using, 106–108
  communicating. *see* communicating
    evidence
  comparisons between observations, 92–95
  comparisons over time, 90–92, 98–99
  comparisons with, combining, 95–101
  difference-in-differences analysis, 96–101
  disaggregating, 89
  distribution of, 87
  goal-setting using, 88–89
  mean (average) of, 86
  median of, 87
  outliers in, 105–106
  percent change versus percentage point
    change, 100–101
  scatterplots and regression analysis, 101–104,
    124, 127–129
  simplifying, 86–89
  survey data, using, 108–109
  tabular structure for, 85–86
data displays
  bar charts, 124, 127–128
  formatting for, 127–129
  line graphs, 124
  pie charts, not recommended, 123, 125
  scatterplots, 101–104, 124, 127–128
  simplicity of, 123–124
  tables, 124, 129–131
  titles for, 126–127
Data Wise Project, 6, 141
Deans for Impact, 80
Death by a Thousand Tables, 90
demonstrable rationale evidence level, 76,
    79–80
design-based alliances, with RPPs, 156
diagnosing a problem
  actionable diagnoses, focusing on, 17–19
  alternative explanations, ruling out, 19
  brainstorming possible causes, 15–17
  data on outcomes, identifying, 14–15

narrowing questions for, 10
questions for, 9–10, 14
root-cause analysis, 13–14
difference-in-differences analysis, 96–101
differences in means regression analysis, 59
disaggregating data, 89
distribution of data, 87

E

EdReports.org, 42
Educate, 38
Education Next, 38
Education Resources Information Center
    (ERIC), 36–37
Education Week, 34, 38
Edutopia, 41
EdWorkingPapers.com, 37
effect size, 65–66, 68–69, 119–120
Elementary and Secondary Education Act
    (ESEA), 73
ERIC (Education Resources Information Center), 36–37
ESEA (Elementary and Secondary Education
    Act), 73
ESSA (Every Student Succeeds Act)
    definition of evidence by, 73–74
    demonstrable rationale evidence level, 76,
        79–80
    levels of evidence defined by, 75–76
    requirements of, compared to WWC, 31
    Section 1003 funds, requirements for, 75
    strong, moderate, or promising evidence
        levels, 75–78
ethically-conducted research, 150–151
Every Student Succeeds Act (ESSA). *see* ESSA
evidence. *see also* data
    communicating, data displays for. *see* data
        displays
    communicating, findings for, 117–122
    communicating, most powerful evidence for,
        114–117
    communicating, overall structure for, 131–134
    definition of, dictionary, 1
    definition of, ESSA, 73–74
    educators' needs for, 1–2, 4
    from existing research. *see* research, existing
    levels of, ESSA, 75–80

ongoing use of. *see* culture of evidence use
research questions answered by. *see* research
    questions
from your own research. *see* research, your
    own
evidence aggregators, 41–43. *see also* What
    Works Clearinghouse (WWC)
evidence-based policy, 1–4. *see also* ESSA; US
    Department of Education
evidence controls. *see* control variables
evidence of no effect, 66
evidence translators, 40–41
examples
    absenteeism. *see* absenteeism example
    academic performance. *see* academic perfor-
        mance example
    choice-based high school example, 81–82
    online credit-recovery classes example, 82
    workforce development. *see* workforce devel-
        opment example
experiment, 59
external researchers, 149–152

F

Family Education Rights and Privacy Act
    (FERPA), 150–151
findings. *see also* evidence
    drafting, 117–122
    as titles for data displays, 126–127
five whys protocol, 16–19

G

goal-setting using data, 88–89
Gonzalez, Maria (math department chair). *see*
    academic performance example
Google Scholar searches, 35–37
Google searches, 34
graphs, 124. *see also* data displays
greetings strategy example. *see* absenteeism
    example

H

"How do I know?" questions. *see* assumptions,
    questioning
Hurling, Lisa (curriculum director). *see* online
    credit-recovery classes example
hypothesis test, 59

I

impact of strategy
  evaluating, 25–26
  narrowing questions for, 10
  process measures for, determining, 24–25
  questions for, 9–10, 26
  research available for, 25
implementation of strategy
  best-case scenario for, 21–22
  feasibility of, evaluating, 23–24
  multiple strategies, considering, 20
  narrowing questions for, 10
  process measures for, determining, 24–25
  questions for, 9–10
  resources required for, 22–24
improvement science, 6
Institute of Education Sciences, 40
interpreting and communicating evidence. *see*
  communicating evidence
interventions. *see* strategies

J

journalists. *see* media
Journalist's Resource, 34–35, 39
journals, academic, 30–31, 37, 40, 44

K

knowledge, checking validity of. *see* assumptions, questioning

L

learning agenda, 144–149
Lincoln School District. *see* absenteeism
  example
line graphs, 124. *see also* data displays
literature reviews, 34–35, 152

M

Marshall Memo, 40
mean (average), 86
means regression analysis, differences in, 59
media, 38–39
median, 87
meta-analyses, 34–35
moderate evidence level, 75–78

N

National Network of Education Research-
  Practice Partnerships (NNERPP), 157
NCLB (No Child Left Behind) Act of 2001, 73
networked improvement communitites, with
  RPPs, 156
NNERPP (National Network of Education
  Research-Practice Partnerships), 157
No Child Left Behind (NCLB) Act of 2001, 73
no evidence of effect, 67
nonacademic research
  overviews of, 34, 44–45
  sources of, 37–44
norm-referenced scores, 107
norms, organizational, 140–141

O

observations, 85, 92–95
online credit-recovery classes example, 82
opportunity costs, 22
organizational use of evidence. *see* culture of
  evidence use
outliers in data, 105–106
overviews of research
  academic, 34–35
  nonacademic, 34, 44–45
  systematic, 31–33, 44

P

peer review process, 30–31
percent change versus percentage point change,
  100–101
Phi Delta Kappan, 38
philanthropic organizations, 43–44
pie charts, 123, 125. *see also* data displays
pilot tests, 141–143
place-based alliances, with RPPs, 156
Plan-Do-Study-Act, 6, 85
plots. *see* data displays
policies. *see* ESSA; strategies
practical significance, 67–69
practices. *see* strategies
problems of practice
  defining, 11–13
  diagnosing. *see* diagnosing a problem

researching. *see* research, existing; research, your own
strategies for. *see* strategies
process measures, 24–25
professional associations, 38
programs. *see* strategies
promising evidence level, 75–78
p-values, 66, 68–69

Q
qualitative research, 59, 81–82
quantitative studies
  convincingness of. *see* convincingness of research
  ESSA levels requiring, 80
  findings based on, communicating, 117–118, 121, 122
  meta-analyses for, 34
  relevance of. *see* relevance of research
quasi-experimental methods, 62–63, 76
questions
  for best-case implementation scenario, 21–22
  for diagnosing a problem, 14, 15–16
  for evaluating impact, 26
  five whys protocol, 16–19
  questioning assumptions, 11, 86, 140–141
  for research. *see* research questions

R
randomized controlled trial (RCT), 59, 61–62, 76
Regional Education Laboratories, 40
regression analysis and scatterplots, 101–104, 124, 127–129
relevance of research
  criteria for, 47, 50–52
  evaluating based on other variables, 51, 55–56
  evaluating based on outcomes, 50, 54–55
  evaluating based on sample, 51, 56–57
  evaluating based on setting, 51, 57–58
  evaluating based on strategy, 50, 52–54
  subjective perspective for, 47–48
replication crisis, 30

research, basic, 80–81
research, existing
  academic overviews of, 34–35
  academic sources of, 35–37
  appropriateness to your circumstances, 48–49
  citations for, following, 36, 44, 45
  convincingness of, criteria for, 47–48, 68–69
  convincingness of, evaluating, 58–69
  ESSA requirements for, 73–78
  finding, process for, 44–45
  nonacademic overviews of, 34, 44–45
  nonacademic sources of, 37–44
  peer review process for, 30–31
  practical significance of, 67–69, 82–83
  reading regularly, 139
  relevance of, criteria for, 47–48, 50–52
  relevance of, evaluating, 50–58
  replication crisis in, 30–31
  single study, not relying on, 29–31, 77–78
  systematic reviews of, 31–33, 44, 152
research, qualitative, 81–82
research, your own
  assessment data, using, 106–108
  communicating. *see* communicating evidence
  comparisons between observations, 92–95
  comparisons over time, 90–92, 98–99
  comparisons with, combining, 95–101
  data from, analyzing. *see* data
  difference-in-differences analysis, 96–101
  disaggregating data, 89
  ESSA's demonstrable rationale criteria for, 76, 79–80
  evidence from, communicating, 79
  goal-setting using, 88–89
  ongoing examination of effects for, 79
  ongoing use of. *see* culture of evidence use
  outliers in data, 105–106
  percent change versus percentage point change, 100–101
  scatterplots and regression analysis, 101–104, 124, 127–129
  simplifying data, 86–89
  survey data, using, 108–109

research, your own, *continued*
   tabular structure for, 85–86
   when to use, 85–86
research director, 154–156
researchED, 41, 45
researchers
   academic websites of, 37
   cognitive bias of, 30
   contacting directly, 37, 49
   external, 149–152
   research directors, 154–156
   research-practice partnerships (RPPs),
      156–157
   reviews by, 44
   vendors as, 40
research-practice partnerships (RPPs),
   156–157
research questions
   assumptions about, questioning, 11
   learning agenda for, 144–149
   narrowing, 10
   prioritization matrix for, 147–148
   types of, 9–10. *see also* diagnosing a problem;
      impact of strategy; implementation of
      strategy
resources, for implementation of strategy,
   22–24
reteaching strategy example. *see* academic performance example
Robinson, Jim (school board member). *see*
   choice-based high school example
root-cause analysis, 13–14
RPPs (research-practice partnerships), 156–157

S
scaled scores, 107
scatterplots and regression analysis, 101–104,
   124, 127–129
Scholars Strategy Network, 40
Section 1003 funds, ESSA requirements for, 75
selection bias, 60–65, 68–69, 76, 78, 95
simplifying data, 86–89
Sisti, Rebecca (superintendent). *see* absenteeism example

stand-alone literature reviews, 34–35
standardized tests, 106–108
statistical insignificance, 66–67
statistical significance
   definitions and criteria for, 66–68, 68–69
   ESSA requirements for, 74, 76, 77
strategies
   impact of, evaluating. *see* impact of strategy
   implementation of, assessing. *see* implemen-
      tation of strategy
   reviews of, 31–33. *see also* research, existing
   types of, 9
   vendors providing, 3, 20
strong evidence level, 75–78
studies, individual. *see also* research, existing
   academic overviews of, 34, 45
   definition of, 77
   not relying on only one, 29–31
   well-designed and well-implemented, crite-
      ria for, 77
   WWC's reviews of, 32–33
survey data, 108–109
systematic reviews, 31–33, 44, 152

T
tables
   data displays using, 124, 129–131
   tabular data, 85–86
Taylor, Dwayne (chief state school officer). *see*
   workforce development example
"The Science of Learning," 80
think tanks, 39–40
titles for data displays, 126–127
t-tests, 59, 67

U
Usable Knowledge, 40
US Department of Education
   ERIC sponsored by, 36–37
   guidance on ESSA, 77–78
   guidance on Title I funds, 24
   Institute of Education Sciences, Regional
      Education Laboratories, 40
   Institute of Education Sciences, WWC, 1

V

variables, 85
vendors
    programs and strategies by, 3, 20, 22–24
    as source of research, 40
    WWC information regarding, 32

W

What Works Clearinghouse (WWC), 31–33,
    58–59
who-what-when-where-how questions, 21–22
workforce development example
    diagnosing a problem, 14–15, 19
    impact evaluation questions, 26
WWC. *see* What Works Clearinghouse